Be Still the Dawn

DIANN FARNSLEY

WESTBOW
PRESS®
A DIVISION OF THOMAS NELSON
& ZONDERVAN

WestBow Press books may be ordered through booksellers or by contacting:

WestBow Press
A Division of Thomas Nelson & Zondervan
1663 Liberty Drive
Bloomington, IN 47403
www.westbowpress.com
1 (866) 928-1240

THE HOLY BIBLE, NEW INTERNATIONAL VERSION®, NIV® Copyright © 1973, 1978, 1984, 2011 by Biblica, Inc.® Used by permission. All rights reserved worldwide.

ISBN: 978-1-5127-8558-6 (sc)
ISBN: 978-1-5127-8557-9 (e)

Library of Congress Control Number: 2017907280

Print information available on the last page.

WestBow Press rev. date: 5/25/2017

Dedication

To my mother,
For her inspiration and encouragement,
Her patience and unconditional love and care.

To my readers,
In stillness may you find your inner peace.
May you journey with faith, hope, and love.

Thanks

Special thanks to those who worked behind the scenes to help bring
Be Still the Dawn to fruition.

Contents

Introduction 1

Be Still, Everybody Hurts 7

Be Still and Know 87

Be Still the Dawn 183

Epilogue 276

Introduction

Welcome to a journey to walk with steps of faith. My hope is to open your senses to inspiration and imagination.

I'm excited that you're reading this poetic memoir. My poetry dates back to my teenage years. I call my poems "ode-votionals." These poems are odes that are thought-provoking messages and devotions to help promote your self-reflection and growth.

As you read this memoir, think about how you may grow not only spiritually but also emotionally, mentally, and physically. I emphasize your building a relationship with God.

My goal is to speak to you gently like a guide and friend as I invite you on a journey to "be still." Notice the personal touches that reflect pain, joy, and other emotions.

Think back on your life and your experiences. Spend quiet moments taking a walk down your memory lane. Cherish a spontaneous thought that says, "I remember when …"

No matter what your age, may this book remind you of the steps you've taken, the position where you currently stand, the future steps you would like to take, and dreams you would like to realize.

Throughout this book are 333 poems, 3 of which are in this introductory section. My original plan was to compose 365 odes, one for each day of the year. As I drafted the first poem in this section, it spoke to me with meaning, message, and significance. The number 333 summed up what I wanted to say so fittingly.

Let's begin with a vision of stillness and meditate a few moments on the following Bible verses, which invite us to follow the Lord's chosen paths.

Psalm 23:1–3 says, "The Lord is my shepherd, I lack nothing. He makes me lie down in green pastures, he leads me beside quiet waters, he refreshes my soul. He guides me along the right paths for his name's sake."

333

One book of rhymes.
Three sections: "Be Still."
Three hundred thirty-three poems
Manifesting my heart's desires and my will.

Poems dating back
To days in my parents' home
While I was yet a teenage girl
And not yet on the roam.

Well, many years have passed
As I've kept my passion alive,
Thinking, feeling, writing
What messages I care thrive.

For my desire as you read,
For you to think and feel.
If I can evoke thoughts and emotions,
Then this opus is meaningful and real.

Additionally and significantly,
As you read 333,
I chose 3 sections for Jesus,
Who died and rose again at age 33.

I chose the book's title *Be Still the Dawn* many years ago. This memoir characterizes the central message to seek and find. Don't read ahead, as I will later reveal why this title is significant and precious to my heart.

Be Still the Dawn is meant to be read as one large story from front to back. Interlaced with prose and biblical Scripture, this story takes you from feeling the discomforts of pains and struggles to the happiness and joys of realizing your life as God's gift to you.

In "Be Still, Everybody Hurts," imagine that you feel the gentle stream of a river flowing across your feet as you tread rock to rock. You seek private contemplation time when you're hurting.

In "Be Still and Know," you may be seeking a new opportunity through an open door ahead, but you see an open Bible instead. The Bible becomes your open door and invitation to forge a deeper relationship with God.

In "Be Still the Dawn," you are ready for change. You're ready to be restored. You've heard God's whispers and callings. Imagine yourself feeling the ocean tide as it serenely flows over your bare feet and beautiful conch shells embedded in the sand. You feel a greater sense of inner peace as you've allowed yourself to journey with steps of faith.

As you read ahead, relate the following verse to your journey to seek and find. When you have completed this memoir in its entirety, revisit this verse and reflect on the message that God and Christ restore you.

First Peter 5:10 says, "And the God of all grace, who called you to his eternal glory in Christ, after you have suffered a little while, will himself restore you and make you strong, firm and steadfast."

I personally find poetry writing to be an excellent means of self-communication. I encourage everyone to write what he or she thinks and feels at any given moment. The words don't need to rhyme. Be as creative as you like. Seeing your very own thoughts in black and white will be quite self-revealing. Self-reflection is a time of stillness to discover more about yourself.

Be Still in Vision

Let me be a visionary,
Creating vision in ode,
A story filled with "ode-votionals."
This gift I have bestowed.

An "ode-votional" is a devotional
Written poetically
With undertones of insight,
Creative rhymes for you and me.

The art of this writing process
Is therapeutic for the mind,
Looking inward, projecting outward
On a deep level of personal kind.

As you read through the vision,
This book in its entirety,
Think about your own growth
And where you'd like to be.

Be still and know with purpose—
We all survive hurts and pains.
Be still and find your purpose—
Happiness dawns in secret plains.

To capture the essence of an "ode-votional," I gave enhanced meaning to the word *ode*. May an ode *offer deep* experiences. Isn't life one big journey of experience after experience?

Ode-Votional

O—Devotional,
Ode—Votional.
Devotions with emotions, I share; I care
To bring you these odes to:
*O*ffer
*D*eep
*E*xperiences
While you are:
Hurting "still,"
Learning "still,"
Dawning "still,"
Always growing:
Breathing "still,"
Living "still,"
Acting "still."
Perhaps awaiting a time of revelation
Be it so divine,
A brand-new awakening, like a *dawn*
When glory is all thine!

I now invite you to read on and "be still." *Still* sounds rather inactive, but is it really? Treasure stillness, learn how active "still" can be, and then move forward to experience many new awakenings, many new dawns.

Be Still

In Your
Hurting Place

Be Still, Everybody Hurts

Hurts. Pains. Struggles. No matter how you say it, any form of distress is simply not fun. We don't feel good. We seek healing and comfort. We long for happy days. Everybody hurts.

In this section, I both generalize and individualize where I use the words *I* and *me*. We are all unique, yet we share the same emotion that hurt feels uncomfortable.

Hurts and challenges feel dark. It is important that we don't lose sight of light. Think of light as "hope."

Remember the word *hope* as an acronym to emphasize help, openness, praise, and evocation. When you finish this section and move to the next, come to realize the following:

There is *h*elp for your crying heart.
You can feel more relieved when you *o*pen your senses.
You can feel less alone and more secure when you *p*raise God.
When you trust, you *e*voke thought and emotion.

You find compassion for your own self, and you find compassion for others. Doesn't it feel good to have empathy? Empathy is the ability to identify with another's feelings. Some call this putting yourself in another's shoes. Another way is to walk the walk of another.

Since we all hurt, we all can name many times when we wanted a circumstance to turn around into a better chance. Think of this as walking right out of those shoes where you felt a time of pain and slipping right into a comfortable pair that felt much more fitting. Suddenly the frown you once wore turned into a smile. You saw a difference in yourself. And guess what? Others noticed too.

As you read this section, notice several personalized comments regarding what I learned about a given poem. I don't look at everything the same way today as I did yesterday. That is called "change" and "personal growth." We all perceive differently. Let your perception be your own.

You will relate to some poems more than others. You may find a key one that sums up your life at this very moment, and it may stick in your mind. That is a good thing since it is very important to learn from others.

Everybody hurts, and everybody has a story to share. Isn't sharing wonderful? Where would we be without shared hurts and victories?

I open this section with a poem to tie all three sections of this memoir together. Dawn is realization. Reality changes. Each day is new. Each day is a new dawn.

If you hurt now or recall a hurting time, remember that today is a clean and fresh new slate. What can you do to make it so great?

Stitch It Up

Be still, everybody hurts,
A bit broken like slitted shirts.

Or hurting, wearing jagged, torn britches
Reflective of a heart that so needs stitches.

Be still and know that hurt does mend.
Know your God is your best friend.

So give me thread, and I will sew
Stitching words; a story I'll sow.

Over time, I've prayed for words to rhyme,
So in this prayer, I thread this time.

Now is the time to thread and seam
The story line in paper's ream.

The thread will be in black and white.
Be Still the Dawn is mine to write.

The following poem is one of my firsts. I wrote it during young adulthood when I was being true to myself and pursuing higher educational goals. Today I would say accept the past and that some things are final. God may have a plan for your future that far exceeds any past victory or loss you have experienced.

I encourage you to seek God's will and have courage when you fail. Later, you will really appreciate your successes.

Why

Sometimes I sit and wonder why
Life seems that it is passing me by.
Why can't I seem to ever achieve
The hopes and dreams that I believe?

I have a lot. Can't they see?
I only want the best for me.

And though sometimes scared to take a chance,
I'm caught up in the same old dance.

So once again I'll think things out,
Wondering what life is all about.

And if I rise or if I fall,
I must accept the final call.

For what I say and what I do,
I trust myself deep down and true.

I've learned to sort the truth from lies.
Will I further question answers in disguise?

Along similar lines as the last poem, I wrote the next one in my early adulthood days of finding where I fit in. I realized I was growing and changing in a world certainly different than my teenage years in the comfort of my parents' home. In its closing lines, I emphasize individuality. Isn't it important to be your own person and for others to value who you are?

Sometimes I Question

Sometimes good,
Sometimes bad.
At times I'm very happy.
But then again I'm sad.

Sometimes right,
Sometimes wrong.
At times I feel accepted.
But do I really belong?

I'm changing on the outside,
Inside, growing evermore.
Sometimes I sit and wonder
What the future holds in store.

I know today's the moment.
I live for here and now.
To never have all the answers,
Guess I've realized this somehow.

And though always, never, sometimes
It seems I question me.
For you to be you and me to be me
Is a fact that's meant to be.

I wrote the next poem while at my first job after graduating from college. I grew up in the rural countryside, and the newness and strangeness of a big city challenged me. Do you remember a time when you felt like hiding and weren't sure you were going to fit in?

She

She hides like a young, naïve girl.
Maybe that's who they all see.
But she emanates her strength inside
To be the woman who she be.

She trusts in her instincts
To tell her right from wrong.
She lets her conscience be her guide.
Her heart and mind rule strong.

So to be her own best friend
As she grows and changes,
She'll take it one day at a time
To meet what God arranges.

Could this have been you, too, seeking others for fellowship and understanding?

You

You hide like a child at heart.
Maybe that's who they all see.
But you emanate your strength inside
As you stand there right before me.

You never needed my touch
Or the holding of my hand,
Just to hear my friendly voice;
Somehow you understand.

So to be the friend you need
As you're facing something new,
Take it step by step and day by day.
Inner peace will come to you.

Were you perhaps a wallflower, shy and waiting to blossom?

Wallflowers Waiting

Some flowers show up in lonely places,
Sitting empty in idle spaces.

The flowers are not real flowers at all.
They're simply wallflowers who sit at the wall.

Sitting quiet, shy, and meek,
What is it they covet and seek?

Perhaps it seems like waiting games
Till favor comes to oblige their names.

Perhaps they were taught to be seen, not heard,
That silence is golden like a muted word.

While the extrovert may be read like an open book,
The introverted wallflower is hard to hook.

Quiet and mysterious, unpopular some say;
A budding wallflower awaits a pay-off day.

Have you had deep moments of self-consciousness and had to bounce back from embarrassment?

Summon Me

Embarrassing moments can make us unsure
Or summon us forward to try yet once more.

Self-consciousness is hard to deny.
What's the worst you can lose
If you don't ever try?
Efforts, rewards,
Feeling the pains.
Losses and wins,
Reaping the gains.

So you tried again; now you are proud,
Summoned out of the embarrassing shroud.

Perhaps you had to bounce back when facing adversity.

Bounce Back

In the face of adversity,
Stay strong to bounce back.
Face the tribulation
With perseverance as your track.

To surrender to God
When He has your back,
To lead you on a pathway
Of victory and comeback.

God's plans are to prosper
And not live in pain.
Must trust and have faith
The future shall bring gain.

Did you want to escape intimidation from someone you wished would change his or her ways?

The Circle of Peace

Bullies, oppressors, intimidators,
Pressing instigators.

Won't you opt to positively choose?
What more can you possibly lose?

Turn over a new leaf.
Stop causing pain and grief.

For from everyone you've taken
And whose nerves you have shaken,
May you realize you have made mistakes,
Held regrets; so slam on the brakes.

A day you say I want to give,
And that's a healthier way to live.

For when you offer peace to one you call "friend,"
You make peace with your inner self in the end.

Has your inner self been a bit troubled with low self-esteem? Low self-confidence? Did others seem aloof and sometimes make you feel outshined?

One Solitary Weed

Today my view is that of a weed,
A single blade of grass standing in need,
Unscathed by those who trimmed the lawn,
Blowing in the wind, awaiting the dawn.

Fearful that others may cut me down
With a huge grass trimmer of green and brown.
It's quiet at night, people at rest.
I stand here solitary on a hilltop crest.

I long for the company of the flowers and corn.
Their attractiveness outshines a weed and the thorn.
But maybe tomorrow I will be spared
As I was pardoned today.
The flowers and corn may get chosen first,
But the least has much to say.

Have you ever felt driven, like you had to prove something to yourself and others?

As the Dust Settles

Is it a calling or fixation that is driving you?
Is it impulse or obsession you are driving to?
As you feel impelled to act quickly,
Like a cannon in your mind
That catapults sensations
That you just can't leave behind.
For once the dust settles
From the cannon shot before,
It recharges and recatapults
As you react once more.
Over and over again
Like a military's marching order,
Something drives you forward
During such confused disorder.
Don't discount that God could be
Calling you through the dust,
As each dust pile is settling,
Calling you to more deeply trust.

Perhaps you went through a period of doubting support from others. Maybe a mother stepped in to give you an important reminder.

From Daughter to Mother and Back

The steps go higher, higher.
When will I reach the top?
The journey is not easy,
But never will I stop.

I'm driven ever stronger.
I don't know what I'll find.
The best is yet to come my way
Beyond the days behind.

I say hello to the new,
Good-bye to the old.
The pages I turn one by one,
A new story to unfold.

Then I hear somebody say, "Wait!"
It's the voice of my mother.
"Give it time, and it will come.
Look to the help of another.
Live today for today.
Don't worry about tomorrow.
The love you give will be returned.
Don't fill your life with sorrow."

Maybe a father provided some very important words.

An Ode to a Son

"Remember, dear child, life is not easy.
God will test you in good and bad times.
He wants you to be strong, a man of great will."
These words from thy father, he chimes.

Did the son listen?
Let me say more.
He was closed to the truth.
His play was his way,
Blinded by temptation
That led him astray.

Answers there be, but questions he found.
Where was God in his time of need?
"Beside you, dear boy, but you didn't heed."

And so the son went on,
Pondering what he'd done,
Finding faith in God;
He found the truth, the One.

Maybe you found a mentor to give you words of advice.

The Mentor Said

"Hang in there. Stick to the script."
What does the latter tell us
If the former is, "Don't be whipped"?
Day to day is not written
Like evolving movie plots.
Next steps are not preoutlined
Like a puzzle to connect the dots.
Perhaps a script is your chartered path,
From which you don't veer far.
To dramatically change course in the middle
May send you sailing afar.
We often hear the words
"Don't fix what is not broken."
So carefully think before you act,
A mentor has so spoken.

Whoever shared important advice may or may not have swayed you at that point in time. You still felt alone. Right or wrong, you felt this way. You questioned, "Could there be a better way?" You simply felt alone.

To Stand Alone

My eyes are filled with pain.
My heart is bound with fear.
As frozen as I stand there,
I cannot shed a tear.

I see you looking at me,
Then turn your head away.
I'm drifting further from you
With each and every day.

Hanging on to what is lost
Could only be a wrong,
For I know the answers lie
Within my heart, where they belong.

And now as I feel stronger,
Ready to rise above the rest,
I'm challenged as I realize
I must face my greatest test.

I break the shell I live in,
All hardened with clay and stone,
To live my life and dream my dreams,
Whether or not I stand alone.

You didn't want to be alone, yet you kept asking, "Am I needed?"

Puddles

Have you ever felt like you're not needed
And you are just taking up space,
While all the while other persons
Seem content with the daily pace?

And you sit back so quietly,
Frozen, almost numb,
Wondering if you'd be missed
If you would so succumb
To disease, injury, tragedy,
Or some unfortunate fate
That parted you from those you knew
Before life felt so sedate.

Quiet and uneventful
Or characteristically dull
Is how you'd describe the moment
Within your brain and skull.

Pressuring you to seek and find
Warmth of any kind,
To melt your frozen stature
Of ice you wish to fracture.

For if you could only melt,
Maybe others would see your puddles,
Your icy rains that harden you
As you seek friendly hugs and huddles.

You were searching.

In Search of a Friend

Should I ask for a needle and thread
To sew wounds that openly bled?
At times, life seemed like jury and trial.
At times, that sadness was present-day style.

When no action seemed it could right a wrong,
When the voice only sang melancholy song,
Feeling the future might not heal the past.
Knowing life's short and the sky overcast—
Clouds on some days when the heart sought light.
Rain from those clouds impeded your sight.

Somewhere beyond the down-pouring rain
Lies an answer to shield the pain.
Far beyond our visual perception
Dwells a power to erase all deception.

But He must be invited inside
To be your healer and ultimate guide
At times when needle and thread just won't mend
A weary soul in search of a friend.

You searched for a friend who wouldn't reject you and would make you feel important.

Whenever, Wherever

Big or small,
Rejection hurts all.
We say our whys
And hurt from replies.

When someone didn't stand by your side,
Sacrifice time, run to us when we cried.

When someone didn't show up on an important day;
Did his or her own thing, then spoke back with cliché.

"I was busy" is one of those phrases;
So cliché—we have our own paraphrases
That we woefully give back
When we hurt from rejecter's slack.

"How could you forget me that day?"
Isn't that a line the hurt one would say?

If the hurt could then don a new dress
And show another in a way to express,
How blue is the spirit that shines on the face
Like the flowers so blue that sit in a vase.

Then the forgottens would give away blue
Forget-me-not flowers from their point of view.
The flowers that mean, "Remember me forever,"
Hopes for the future
Whenever, wherever.

You sought a friend who will not let you down.

Matchless

Where there's hurt, there's pain,
Longing to be healed.
Where there are wounds, there are scars,
Visible, not concealed,
Open to you and those knowing you best,
For they feel for you and endure the test.

For no one bears personal pain alone
As long as others care.
That's what makes relationships
The dressings that you wear.

Casts and bandages are meant to bind a sore.
Without invitation, you walked through my door.
You are a matchless dressing I've found.
A friend who does not let me down.

You were hurting.

Some Hurting Place

To have cried
Says I've tried
To be strong
Far too long.
To have wept
Says I've kept
Feelings bound
So profound.

That cut so deep
And run so wide
And cross right back
To the other side,
Propelling and swelling
The tears down my face.
Each watery drop
Relieves some hurting place.

You felt immersed in a sea of tears.

Tears in the Sea

Out of touch with reality,
Drowning in a stormy sea,
Too weak to swim to land afar,
How is it I came this far?
Trying hard so very long
To be vigorous and strong.
Am I weakened by my tears?
Those held back for many years.
Am I brave to let tears flow?
One by one, they overflow.
Perhaps I am this very day
To preserve my life at bay,
So seawaters do not grow
With my tears mixed in the flow.

You hoped God would deliver His touch and the right people into your life to stay for the long ride.

Hold His Touch

When there are no outstretched arms before you
For comfort and consolation,
You may feel pining for a touch
To relieve the desolation.

You are always touched by God's everlasting arms.
They encircle you for safety from real and perceived harms.

Although you cannot see His arms,
May you hold His touch within your mind.
Experience divine communion,
An invisible bond like no other kind.

Then hold steadfast to faith that God will deliver to you
Wonderful, divine connections, the right people just for you.

When right people cross your path
Unexpectedly or through friendship over years,
They will be the ones who stay
And willingly share your tears.

You sought safe people to tell your secrets to and to communicate with integrity.

The Latest and the Greatest

The latest and the greatest—
Have you heard the latest?

News travels fast
By numbers, oh so vast,
Through the rumor mill telephone line,
By the ever-twisting gossip grapevine.

By do tellers who will tell
And listeners who retell.
The story that is stretched
Becomes a tale farfetched,
Traveling grapevines from
Arbor to arbor,
Twisting its way to
Some faraway sea harbor.

The latest and the greatest—
Have you harbored the latest?

Kept my secrets for me,
My confidant and friend.
A vine ran from me to you,
And you were the vine's end.

Be my safe harbor,
Not my grape arbor,
Where stories travel vines
And become twisted untruth lines.

A time of comfort felt so long overdue.

Long Overdue

When you once held back
And tried to be brave,
Resisted vulnerability
As if tears could not save.

When you thought a brave face
Was expected and right,
And feared looking weak
Was not a good sight.

When you've held within
Year after year,
Wanting dry cheeks,
Not the wet drip of tears.

Then you reach a point,
A junction one day,
When you really feel
What it's like to be gray.

Knowing you've run and run away.
Run till you're ready and not led astray
By your own attitude.
Will it punish or reprieve?
Rely on others and come to believe;
They'll let your tears flow, and they'll offer to dry
The long-overdue wetness that flows from each eye.

You dried crying eyes with many tissues.

Tissues

Everybody cries.
Everyone has whys.

There's time for healing.
It's part of real feeling.

No matter how many tissues it takes,
Don't speed up the process.
Just put on the brakes.

Learn from your issues
And all the wet tissues.

Dry eyes will greet you
In the mirror one day,
A day you moved forward
And tucked issues away.

It struck you deeply. Everybody has issues.

Issues

Are we ordinary people with extraordinary issues?
Or extraordinary people with ordinary issues?

However you say it, both apply.
We're all people with issues,
And we will get by.

Hurt fills life, but hurt is a time to show care.

Scars, Wounds, Triggers, Time

Scars, wounds, triggers, and time,
All set to words in rhyme.

A scar may show.
A wound may heal.
A trigger may resurface,
And time will reveal.

The invisible plot,
Much like a plan,
That only God knows,
Unfolding for man.

Where man is all, not one certain one.
Plans for all men, just like Holy Son,

For Jesus assuredly said,
"They know not what they do."
We've all been hurt by some,
Rarely just a few.

At times we hurt others,
Forgetting our brothers.
At times we face twisters,
Forgetting our sisters.

At times we hurt self,
Our very own pride.
At times we hurt groom.
At times we hurt bride.

Hurt fills life.
It's all around.
But feeling hurt,
Now that's profound.

Hurt is care.
Care is a bond.
A bond is a blessing.
The reality has dawned.

Showing and receiving care is a delicate balance. We all need a certain level of independence and balanced relationships that feel healthy. Sometimes this means loving from a distance.

From Latch to Detach

When we people latch,
We tend to attach.
When we people love,
We feel free to detach.

Detachment is not painless,
But may help two's sanity.
Responding with compassion,
Not acting out with vanity.

It is hard to manage and draw a fine line_____
Between dynamics of selfishness and selflessness,
To care with loving *d-i-s-t-a-n-c-e*
But not take on another's distress.

For we are all needy people
Who vary in our needs.
We desire to be supportive people
Who willingly do good deeds.

But we all have emotions to manage
While averting the path of emotional damage.
What does the path to emotional wellness look like
That strengthens our persona, our very own psyche?

Be optimistic about your life.
Approach your life with good attitude.
Encourage others to treat their lives the same.
Express emotions with suitable habitude.

In other words, be habit forming.
Walk the path of self-awareness.
A detaching habit is a good habit
To care with distance and fairness.

Life starts to feel like harmony.

Fantastically

Loose as a gypsy running wild.
Tight as a puppet on a string.
Not wanting to be dangled too freely,
Nor bound in a taut coiled ring.

Neglect will alienate me.
Control will stifle me.

There must be a delicate balance
Of freedom that we share.
When we are parted for a while,
We'll return for sweet affair.

To share the closeness and time
Of good friends in amity,
A harmony that makes us feel
Oh so fantastically!

Reduce your temptation to run wild.

Inner Child

When you feel like running wild,
Relax and find your inner child.

Don't grow up to be grumpy and sour.
Treasure each second, minute, and hour.

Sure, you've witnessed pain over the years,
And sure, you've wiped away crocodile tears.

Displayed emotions sincere like the rest.
Other times simply sought pity at best.

Find a place where you feel innocent and calm.
It's there you'll feel safe in God's gentle palm.

Increase your patience to wait and trust.

Trust Him to Act

Hurry up and wait but wait.
I turn around and more.
Somebody's chasing after me,
Knocking at my door.

So I try to sit tight,
Patient as can be.
Then I turn around to find
Somebody's calling me.

Hurry up. Sit tight.
Do this. Don't be late.
Sit tight. Hurry up.
Do that. Do not wait.

After all is said and done,
Next comes the time-out phase,
To turn around and sit down,
Deal with mindless daze.

Count to ten and stand up.
I turn around and more.
Things start to differ than
They really were before.

There's time to hurry, time to wait;
Time to act, not hesitate.

In a world of hustle,
In a time of bustle,
In a place of flurry,
In an age of scurry.

So count to ten
If you must retract.
It'll be all right.
Trust Him to act.

You face a realization. God wants you to have freedom and balance. He can help stitch and heal.

From Parted Seams to Stitched-Up Dreams

Have to be. Want to be.
Need to be. Like to be.
God, what would You have me be?
God, what would You have me see?

I see visions.
I see dreams.
In times of confusion,
I'm parted at the seams.
So God, I pray for needle and thread.
Stitch me up where anguish once spread.

God walks with you as you feel.

Sorrows Fade Like Ashes' Dust

I may feel worn, forlorn, and torn,
Wishing I could be reborn.

In hard days with my worried face,
I must seek unconditional grace.

The grace that God alone can give
For each and every day I live.

Worry will deter me more,
Undermine faith that should outpour.

For only in my faith and trust
Will sorrows fade like ashes' dust.

God shows you a long ride is durable and real.

A Long Ride

May your dearest friends help weather you through life's storms.
May you nourish and comfort each other, no matter what trial forms.
Victory awaits on the other side of a temporary downslide.
No storm lasts forever when you persevere a long ride.

Has anyone ever so angered you that you just wanted him or her to go? God wants people to stay and work together. God is about reconciliation. He is for REAL.

Let's think about REAL and a spiritual way to be real.

REAL: Reconcile, Erase Anger, Love

Reconcile to God. He will erase anger. You will reap more love for each other and for God too.

For REAL

I wanted you to go.
God wanted you to stay.
You angered me one day.
He took the anger away.

I thought, *Really*!
He thought for REAL!
And now with reconciliation,
His thoughts we feel.

We feel REAL.
We feel blessed.
We've said our thank-yous,
And God takes care of the rest.

Furthermore, have patience when you reconcile. Reconciliations take time.

To Reconcile with Patience

Reconcile first and foremost to God
When your soul is feeling ill.
You will have those very days,
Needing the verse of Psalms, "Be still,"
When stillness is to know Him
When you just can't grasp the scene,
How and when your soul gets well
With patience in the time between.
Patience is a virtue,
For which reconciliation depends.
Have patience and trust in God,
For an ill soul always mends.

Let's turn our attention to the deep hurts of anger. It is important to tame anger before it runs rampant and causes relationship turmoil. Think about how you control anger and how you react to others' anger as you read this section.

To It and Through It

Anger taken out on another;
Momentary rage?
Not your self and character;
Was it just a stage?

If God brought you to it,
He will bring you through it.

The anger you expended,
To your "self" defended?

Did you feel entitled to let things out?
Sometimes cry, and sometimes shout?

To preserve your inner self
And cleanse what felt so bottled;
When after the fact you clearly knew
The behavior you wouldn't have modeled.

But it's done and over with.
Confess to God your part.
God will bring you through it
And cleanse your wayward heart.

Have you allowed your anger to turn into a sea of rage?

Who'll Be Near the Anger Sea?

I guess you could say I caged my rage.
Now it has taken center stage.
Once hidden in the backseat suppressed,
Now it flows; it's not undressed.
The rage is dressed, and it is plain;
Has taken meaning and is hard to wane.

Hard on others who say, "Who's she?"
What has happened, "Who she be?"
Others have not seen this before.
Do we know her anymore?
Is she friend, or is she foe
As we watch her anger blow?
Will she fight, or will she flee?
Feel justified in the anger's sea?

A sea of anger, thundering day and night;
That can knock others down like a drag-down fight.
Is she nice, or is she spice?
Pungent, pervasive, a cutting vice?
But if she's not allowed to vent,
Her life will spin with cruel torment,
With intensity you would not want to feel,
But perhaps you have, if you are real,
For aren't all humans anger prone
When shoved beyond their comfort zone?
When the slightest tick becomes ticked off
And high sensitivity is so hard to doff?
Will her sensitivity wax and wane
Or stabilize to some smooth plane?

Anger in is anger pent.
Anger out is then time spent,
Invested to cleanse the inner soul,
Spent to feel a sense of whole.
Anger in is disarray.
Anger out will fade away.
To a time of renewed healing;
The clock then chimes restored feeling.
With peace and calm, joy and cheer,
I wonder then, *Who'll be near?*

Have you thought about the root causes of your anger? Or about the big mysterious question, "Why?" Have you asked, "Where does my anger take me?"

To Dress Anew

Why do you harbor such anger?
Why do you cling to sorrow?
Can't you see beyond the past?
A present and tomorrow?

Why do you swallow such grief?
Why do you indulge despair?
Won't you heal those deep-felt wounds
Not scarred beyond repair?

You're lost and confused.
Fall back in depression.
Twisted 'round and about,
Not quite grasping progression.

You speak of the dark side.
Well, many don't know.
Those demonic memories—
They are your foe.

Won't you speak of white,
Like heaven's grains of sands?
Black and white do fight
Like two not holding hands.

Oh, let the rain fall down in drenches.
Wash away sins; pull out of the trenches.

As you battle within,
Then you become gray.
Can't you see others
Looking concerned in dismay?

White is not perfect and never will be.
In the absence of light,
Black and gray do blind me.

No matter what the mirror shines,
Sing, "I am good inside.
I was made in God's image.
The dress is on the outside."

The dress can't be preserved in a box,
Like a tangible memory.
But the spirit in your soul
Can surely set you free.

The dress might lose its color one day,
As life is ever changing.
To never be exactly who we were,
God knows what He's arranging.

He'll not mind if you dress anew.
God is looking out for you.

The next few poems focus on communication with one another. Let them guide and help you find an important soft spot within your heart. Let hardness soften. God has so commanded us to love our neighbors as ourselves.

Guided Accord

God, grant us softer hearts,
For being mad is like throwing darts.
One throws a word, then the other back.
Each other combats an emotional attack,
As if to avoid the other's bull's-eye,
Where a pointed pierce hits the heart on a try.
For words can hurt, and words do sting
Much more than fists that hurl and sling.
So when anger feels like you're shooting a dart board,
Sense a person who can be wounded by misguided discord.

Look at the big picture, the vast landscape, and the view you help paint.

A Blemished Landscape

Don't let my actions scar you. You know I have some pressure.
For if you care unconditionally, tomorrow will be much fresher.

I know I've said and done some things that I so regret.
In the heat of a stressful moment, I wish I could forget.
Everybody does this; no one escapes transgressions.
But work harder the next time and focus on progressions.

When you're weary, don't grow faint.
The landscape is yours to color and paint.
With sunny hues or darkened blues,
Light, bright colors you may choose.

Don't let your heart grow hard as stone.
Work to heal and softly atone.
Your future landscape may carry a blemish or two,
Which are not troublesome scars for me and for you.

When it comes to anger and other strong emotions, have you ever repressed them? Have you tried so hard to be kind that you stored away very strong feelings and resentments to a deeper part of your mind, which you may refer to as the "back stage"?

The Back Stage

I felt like I chose a target that day,
Someone standing in my way,
As I felt internal anger and rage
Hurling from a repressed back stage,
A stage I kept buried in my mind;
Year after year, pain so confined.
That wasn't released timely with incidence
But now pervades more than coincidence.

For old hurts and wounds have refestered,
And my spirit and ego feel so pestered.

With torment and plague,
That's more than vague.
It's sharp and pointed
As I come disjointed.
I feel the depression
Caused by repression.
Consciously aware,
It hit me so square.
How deep did my thrust
Diminish our trust?
How deep did my stage
Fester your rage?

Now we are quiet
To avoid backlash.
Repression is not good,
Those memories we stash.

Repression released
Is now unleashed,
Like the taming and capture
Of some wild beast,
A beast not settling
In the back stage of your mind
When you walk with your friend
From a cage once confined.

While letting repression go, you released pent-up, wounded feelings, startled others, and were afraid of how they would react. Would they simply turn their backs and walk away?

Blessed with Hearts

I'm playing with a full deck,
Fully aware of my hurts.
My cards are all on the table.
I've shed my holey shirts.

Where past triggers fired
And went deeper than outerwear,
It's likely you can't take
My wounded feelings that I share.

I fully expect you to leave
As I've been letting repression go.
But when I felt unconscious,
I was a comatose ego.

Living day by day
As if I could quell real pain,
Denying the reality
As if I lived in a fast lane.

For when that lane got slow
And time caught up with me,
I came to realize
The pains of memory.

Now my full deck of cards
Only contains the hearts,
The only suit I pulled out
To shuffle and restart.

I discarded the clubs,
Much like leafy clover.
I need more than luck
To proceed in my makeover.

I discarded the spades,
As I'm not fond of black.
The color is the absence of light,
So it restricts how I bounce back.

I discarded the diamonds,
For I'm not made of glass.
All that is left are hearts,
The tender center of mass.

Fifty-two hearts in my new deck;
No joker to be wild.
With that many hearts supporting me,
I'm such a "bless-ed" child!

If fears and issues trouble a couple, has the relationship become competitive?

As the Smoke Clears

When peace and power compete,
Love starts to sour as forces divide.
As forces rival and challenge more,
The split grows ever so wide.

Like a chasm, a deep fissure in the earth,
Creating a deep ravine;
Profound differences between people
Are a chasm much like a smoke screen.

Perhaps one or both
Are afraid of what they think and feel,
As if they've hidden behind a smoke screen
And can't recognize what is real.

Any such screen, like smoke, will clear.
Close the chasm with less defense.
Speak clarity and find similarity.
The dust settles when the smoke's less dense.

As two feel tested, allow openness to bind and start with a positive mind. Be thankful and practice having an attitude of gratitude.

Two Softened Hearts

The heartbreak of couples disengaging;
Seems their love is a trial.
Tested and tested over again,
Maybe they slip back in denial.

They seem to cover surface triggers,
Not root causes from within.
Are they just so different
They forget where to begin?

Casting an aura like a double-edged sword,
Cycling through love and hate,
Projecting negativity and doubts upon the mate.

When they start to look positively,
Leaving options in their minds,
The hearts will welcome new solutions
And an openness that binds.

Recementing a broken bond
Requires engaging, listening, and speaking—
And very importantly, two softened hearts
To rediscover what they are seeking.

Remember, God is there to turn to in times of anger. You may be tempted to feel like others are judging you. Don't we all feel this way sometimes? Are we a bit quick to judge others while not wanting others to judge us?

To God's Command

Don't be a jury of my fury.
Releasing my rage is just a stage.

That I'm in,
Like downcast sin
Pressuring me to get it out
With pouring tears and panic shout.

As if to unchain such a binding shackle,
For my freedom I do tackle.

So I may proclaim,
"I've been set free!
My chains are gone, and I can see!"

The clouds, with a silver lining ahead,
Erasing bad memories that spin in my head.

For even within what seems so bad,
The good will shine to God's command.

When is the time the silver lining shines? Don't we all ask, "When?" and "How much longer?"

When

When does bitterness end?
Foe turn into friend?
God, step into solve
What we can't resolve.

So we can live and thrive,
Not be eaten alive
By nightmares and fears,
Ever-flowing tears,
The kind that tire you out,
Make you want to shout.

Feel like throwing your hand,
Ready to call it quits
When you see no ladder
To rise you from the pits.

You may feel stuck in a trap and sad.
Bang your fists as you are mad.

Scream from your lungs, "No more!"
Where from the roof down to the floor,
You can't catch a breath of fresh air
When every breath is just despair.

When your breath starts to feel like care and not despair, you look through the eyes of a beholder. You witness 'me and you' and 'you and me' and understand relationships flow both ways. So behold one another, yet realize that nothing is too difficult for God.

Behold

There's a 'me and you' in what we do,
A 'me and you' in what we say.
In times of my struggles, dependence leans to you.
Symmetrically with my stumbles, support leans my way.

There's a 'you and me' in what we do,
A 'you and me' in what we say.
In times of your stumbles, support leans to you.
Symmetrically with your struggles, dependence leans my way.

But importantly there's leaning
And another who offers a shoulder,
Someone sensitive and aware
Peering through the eyes of a beholder.

To behold is a special form of witness,
A beauty between friend and friend.
A single body cannot lean on oneself
But must understand and comprehend.

It's important to behold mankind,
For man is good, and man is kind.

But if anything is too difficult for man,
Our God of mankind declares,
"Nothing is too hard for Me.
Please bring Me your troubles and cares."

Have you ever felt reluctant to let others in and get to know the real you? Social engagement and bonding require intimacy, not hiding behind superficial masks.

The Mask We Wear

Do you wear a mask to shield a pain?
Or bear yourself in the pouring rain?

Do you wear a mask when you are weak?
Hold in your thoughts and dare not speak?

Do you wear a mask to hide some shame
And often refuse to take the blame?

Do you run from finding yourself?
Sit idle like the books on a shelf?

Do you wear a mask once a year
And celebrate with treats and cheer?

Masks on Halloween may be the best,
Those worn in fun times and for zest.
Or perhaps during a party called "the masquerades"
Or playing silly games of guess and charades.

But there are masks of inner defenses,
Confusing and beyond our senses.

Those masks are hard to remove and break
For fear one's impression will be a mistake.

Be careful with the mask you wear,
For inner emotion does easily tear.

Emotion differs from paper-mache,
Even latex and even clay.

Behind a mask
The face tells much more.
Every wrinkle and feature
Has a story in store.

Have you felt split inside as if you have an alter ego? Some second personality that is not your authentic self?

A Mask of Two

I feel what I know not;
It's so hard to define.
I try to understand it,
But questions intertwine.
I know not what I feel;
It's so easy to deny.
I try to understand it,
But it answers only, "Why?"
If it be, then it be so.
If it is not, then just let go.
To bear no lies behind a mask
Is to hide no truth before this task.
I live for me and not for you.
There be it one.
There is no two.

Have you felt confused and torn as if you were observing someone else acting with an alter ego? Some second personality that is not his or her authentic self?

From Ear to Ear

I see one. I hear two.
Two voices in one vision.
Who?
I see two. I hear two.
Two voices in two visions.
Who?

Who are you, and why is this?
Is this a good and evil twist?
One staring face,
One smile, one frown,
Voices warring, neither drown.
Two staring faces,
Both in frown,
Voices warring, won't one drown?
So I may see one smiling face,
One sweet voice to speak with grace.
Facial language, oh let me hear,
A smiling face from ear to ear!

What else weighs you down? What thoughts are you dwelling on that cause you to feel stuck and restless? The next several poems focus on what we think about and how we can be so tempted to give up. Consider your options carefully. Is giving up the answer?

Carefree

A restless mind
Like no other kind.
Unruly, unduly,
Here I say truly.

When the mind is not at rest,
We do not work our very best.

The feet may be weary,
The eyes strained and teary.

Clumsy and stumbling,
One may say "fumbling,"

As if you grasp for straws,
As your deep breath draws.

So as the breath paces,
Feel the mind find peace.
Cease the chases.
Peace builds upon peace.

Isn't it great not to run restlessly?
Letting the mind be uncluttered
With desires carefree.

Are you allowing past memories and rumination to hinder you from living out a more meaningful story?

Memory Sticks to Building Bricks

Have you ever felt burdened by disturbances
You thought were demons for sure?
That lingered in your mind
As you screamed to hear no more?

Have you said, "Is this my conscience
Talking to me somehow?"
Or did your mind drift spookily,
Like the ghosts' voices on the prowl?

Most likely you're just thinking about
The past surfacing from within,
Way below the depths of your triple layer of skin.

Something that is skin deep is not lasting but superficial.
Something that is deep under the skin is no way artificial.

Skin deep is one dimensional, shallow in the mind;
But that which has real meaning is a story of another kind.

Letting go of past disturbances
Makes room for future bricks,
Solid and healthy emotions
More supportive than old fragile sticks.

Building bricks and paving stones,
Building blocks and cornerstones,
Underneath your present two feet
That blot out intrusive memories like treading the key 'delete.'

Is your story feeling more twisted than it was before?

Unravel the Knots

Why does life get twisted even worse than pretzel dough
With knots and bends, uneven curves, dissension that does grow?
When discord lacks harmony and satisfying peace,
It could explode like thunderbolts and lightning to unleash.
So take the discord and unravel every knotted source.
Look closely for the root cause for sadness and remorse.
Sharpen your pencil. Write your thoughts.
Get it out, all of those knots.
Take a deep breath.
Oh, how you sighed,
When knots are loosed
And you're feeling untied.

Have the knots gripped you with agonizing fears? Fears that have turned into storms? You want to stop these storms in their tracks.

Storm Chaser

When all our worst fears materialize,
They brew on the stormy home front.
We experience torrential winds
Like cyclones, twisters, and brunt.

Tornadoes in our minds
Like no precedent of its kind.

Our fears cause us to agonize.
If rampant, they can paralyze.
Have we overanalyzed to death
That it's hard to catch a breath?

What a heavy burden
To carry all those fears.
Did they stop you in your tracks?
Did you wallow in your tears?

If you let your storms chase you,
Chase them right on back.
Be an active storm chaser
And stop them in their tracks.

You want to wake up each morning as if there is a right side, not a wrong side that adds to the day's priorities.

Language of Numbers

Waking up on the wrong side of the bed
Adds a stressor or two.
Soon before you know it,
They've multiplied for you.

Which one do you tackle first?
Which can wait for last?
Hard to be slow and patient;
You want to solve so fast.

Is your plan to divide and conquer?
Subtract them one by one?
Take one away, another returns;
The job seems never all done.

It's hard to relieve our stressors.
This we all do know.
Just a simple fact of life,
An equation outlined in a row.

Sometimes add, sometimes subtract,
Often multiply, then divide.
Round and round, you do the math.
The solution, you decide.

But if you find no answer,
Don't feel that you will fail.
Look to God for prioritization.
His language will help you prevail.

Like hidden probability,
Not random circumstance;
So biblically speaking,
He offers not one but "another" chance.

When feeling overloaded, you want to subdue distressing thoughts that cause more stress.

The Compress

Being restless,
You do rest less,
Feeling the press
Of a flattening compress.

As if the mind is crammed and jammed,
Telling the body it is so slammed.

By incessant thoughts
That drift like a cloud,
Like waves of the ocean,
Crashing in so loud.

Overloading the mind
And its mental filter;
Deluged with notions
That shake you way off kilter.

Some thoughts vibrate quickly,
Then they leave.
Others resonate
Like your heart worn on your sleeve.

Carrying worry around day by day
Will become senseless and deeply ricochet.

A rebounding thought is an inner projectile
That aims and pokes at your very lifestyle.

But everyone carries projectiles, those thoughts
That leave us so pressed and wrapped up in knots.

There's no easy answer to acquire your rest.
But try the following
When you're restlessly stressed.

Decompress, remove the compress,
A very thought that gives you distress.

Stress and inner pressures may feel so marked and defined like wrinkles.

Wrinkles without a Dress

Her hair so neatly tressed in locks.
Her lovely figure dressed in frocks.
But when it comes to how she's pressed,
She squeezes her arms about her chest.

For she knows the wrinkles that you cannot see
In her clothes so pressed,
For she knows the wrinkles that you can see
Are from her life when stressed.

She knows what she can smooth,
The story in her clothes.
She knows what she can't iron,
The story in her woes.

Outside in and inside out,
She knows the intimacy without a doubt.

She's just like you and me,
Troubled at times by what we see,
Wrinkles that we can live without,
Those we can do nothing about.

Our dress, our tress,
Our outerwear
Can be perfected with a press.
But our inner pressures are like
Wrinkles without a dress.

Downheartedness may leave you feeling like you are still but a child who reverts to that stage in your older age.

The Grown-Up Child

A wounded child in grown-up shoes,
Wearing scars and feeling the blues.

Asking for a heart to soften,
To cry less and laugh more often.

A downhearted child in grown-up dress,
Trying to bear life's daily stress.

Asking for a heart to feel
Self-compassion as one kneels.

That emotion merciful and kind
When feeling deranged and losing your mind.

That very friendly act of care
For yourself in loving prayer.

So practice self-compassion today,
To walk in your shoes this grown-up way.

You don't want to feel stuck in a middle place, where you feel you cannot move.

Middleman without a Plan

Soul Master,
Soul Safe Guarder,
When I try hard,
You give harder.

Especially during stresses of life,
When I cry and cry,
Depending too much on myself,
Dearly how I try—
To not bend or snap
When taking others' rap,
When I feel like the middleman
In a middle without a plan.

When something or someone is blocking me
From moving forward and higher.
When I can't escape by lowering
Where backward be blocking brier,

As if I were stuck on a ladder
Somewhere in the middle,
Nowhere to move, nowhere to go,
Just like a second fiddle.

But there's another option;
I can simply jump,
For my Soul Master, Safe Guarder
Catches each bruise and bump.

You don't want to feel trapped in a pit where you feel swallowed.

I Be Doled!

I'm not fond of pits and ruts,
Those big holes that swallow my guts.
Sometimes I sit and stew and wallow
If an issue at hand seems too big to swallow.

Sometimes I bite off more than I can chew
When baby steps can get me through.
Sometimes a tart is better than a pie,
A small portion so doled versus a sandwich piled high.

Life sometimes needs some portion control,
Balance to feel a sense of whole,
To not cling to some unhealthy pit,
But to be consoled by portions that fit.
To fittingly proclaim, "I be so doled!"
Thankfully shout, "I be consoled!"

You want to be strong and not give up. You want to hang in there and hang tight.

Swung from Strand to Rope

Giving up is easy,
And another may understand.
Yet keeping yourself together
Is strength as you hang by a strand.

When you hold on and hold it together,
You now hang by a rope,
Showing others you didn't fall apart
And that you can succeed and cope.

You don't want to feel scattered or like a stray sheep that has lost its identity.

Day by Day

Losing my identity,
Asking, "Who am I?"
How to go on another day
As I curl in a ball so shy.

The night falls.
I cry.
Not tucked in bed,
I spy.

Spying like a secret search
Trying to reveal.
"Where did I go?
God, won't you heal?"

God, you surely know me,
Even when I don't know myself.
Holy and blameless in your sight,
Help me find myself.

Scattered I be like ashes.
Broken I be like glass.
Wounded I be with scars
That are not fading fast.

My soul will never be perfect,
But I will take it cleansed.
Oh, dear Spirit purify me
Like a sheep the shepherd tends.

You want to breathe with ease and rest before you reach a breaking point. Then you say to yourself, "Time out."

Rest before Regrets

I know you know I can,
But I'm feeling like I can't.
This overstretched rubber band
Feels meager and so scant.

What will more pressure do
To my bandwidth and success?
Don't I have a breaking point?
Be it fact or myth.

I say I need to be less taut
Between points *A* and *Z*,
Perhaps to shed some baggage
As I even get to *V.*

W, X, Y, and *Z*
Are adding too much stress.
A little time-out is inviting,
Be it rest before regrets.

The last few pulls may get easier,
As my rubber band's relaxed,
Restored to a comfort zone
And graciously untaxed.

You give yourself time for private contemplation as you are still in your quiet, private space.

Private Contemplation

Ashes from private guilt.
Stains left on the floor.
Teardrops fell there too.
How do I take anymore?

If it's high tolerance and patience
That get me through the day,
Then I thank God for that strength
That carries me on my way.

Don't prey on my weaknesses but pray over them,
As prayers are so lovingly taught in songs and anthems.

Out of weakness arises great strength with time and duration.
Isn't there something mystical about private contemplation?

Devotion with the Lord,
Who sees all these heartfelt stains.
In His perfect timing,
He'll wash them away like rains.

Your floor beneath that you do walk
Won't look so guilty and stained.
Burnt ashes from your private wounds and fires
Will be extinguished and contained.

From that stillness, you meditate on change and say, "I don't want to run around in circles."

Circular Rain

Don't allow your
Cyclical pain
To weight you down like
Circular rain,
Rain that comes
Right back around,
Down pouring heavy,
Just beating the ground.

Other things go round and round
Like blessings that are newly found,
For you are blessed, and pain will fade.
Get out of that rain where you do wade.

Look for insight and depth in what's good,
Then plunge forward from the position you stood.

You desire to think and act smart and to be more self-composed.

Making Sense of Common Sense

Common sense.
If it's common,
Why is it hard to find?
By all people sometimes,
We're just not using our minds.

It wasn't named "rare sense"
To use sparingly once in a while.
It wasn't named "untapped sense"
To be hidden and out of style.

It wasn't termed "street smarts"
Or "smart sense" based on intellect.
No, it's common sense to sense commonly
Like a common dialect.

You start to realize you have been stuck in a dark place that will grow lighter. You seek to navigate to a place for solid support as firm as rock.

The Clam I'm In

My heart bleeds with tears.
My nerves have destabilized.
I really long to be
Energized and mobilized,
To move each day in such motion,
As if I'm not in a gridlock or jam.
To not feel my very flesh
Encased by a burrowing clam.

Oh, that ocean mollusk
That has buried me in the sand,
Diminishing my ability
To stand on solid rock and land.

For sand pulls me down, and rock provides support.
Rock can move me from my place; this I so report.
So God be my rock; break the clam I find myself in.
God, be my healer; mend the jam I feel within.

Your jam and dark place may have felt like a shell encasing your body and spirits.

I challenged myself during those times when I sought to break a shell and receive more light. This poetic memoir is my form of learning, sharing, and investing many hours to compose a story. What shell would you like to break to allow yourself to rise to a new challenge?

The Shell Breaks

If I live within a shell,
Then help me break its crest.
I'm challenged as I realize
I must face a notable test;
To poetically build a story
Like none I've ever penned,
Investing time and commitment
To share with friend and friend.

You start believing turnarounds will eventually happen.

Upshift

Sometimes I feel downhearted by circumstance,
Not easily foreseeing a turnaround chance:

The kind of turnaround that solves a problem completely,
So I can move forward and live very sweetly.

Many times there's distress in a job's assignment.
Mundane be a task, such a boring alignment.

At times I must do what I care not.
Cross the T's, I's I must dot.

To wrap up things and achieve an alignment
Before I progress to the up-turn assignment:

A new circumstance to upturn and uplift,
A turnaround chance so my mood will upshift.

But things may get worse before they get better.

Think Better

As life turns bitter, think better.
It may get worse.
It may get wetter.

The storm may continue a bit longer.
Yet when the sun shines,
You'll be stronger.

Weathering those rains,
Jagged, nagging pains.

When it gets worse before it gets better,
And the sun shines brightly after it rains wetter.

Suddenly, the winds change. Look at what you believe in now.

Winds of Change

Winds of change will blow.
Growing pains will ebb and flow.

Don't let the winds knock you off your feet.
The ground is not your rooted seat,
For low to the ground is like a dark spirit.
Get up, get moving, and just don't be near it.

Raise up, raise high,
Like trees to the sky.
Think victor, not victim,
And battles you'll lick 'em.

As if no wind will sweep you away
Or be so painful to cause dark dismay.

Believe that gusts will thrust you to light
And that you deserve great fortune so bright.

To lighten up your spirit, you might think back to being a young child and hearing comforting words. Perhaps those words came from a teacher.

Boo Bugs

Boo bug. Shoo slug.
Scant ant. I can. You can't.
I'll scare you. You can't scare me.
You won't fret my mind. I'll set you free.

My science teacher said one day,
"We're going to study bugs."
She said, "If you tell me your bugaboo,
Then I will give you hugs."

Next, we spoke of another bug,
The one we called a "bugbear."
She said, "If you tell me yours,
Then mine I will also share."

Teacher said that either bug
May scare, confuse, and annoy.
She said it may feel so huge
To any big or little girl or boy.

The whole class quickly answered,
"Creepy, crawly spiders. Things that go bump in the night.
Those are our bugaboos and bugbears
That chase us under the bed with fright."

The teacher went around the room,
Giving each child a hug.
We all laughed at her simply stated task:
"Just sweep under the rug."

When bugged by bugaboos and bugbears,
Spiders and worries and frights and huge scares,
"Take your broom and with effort sweep.
Clean bugs in your mind that so crawl and so creep."

Teacher ended our class,
Said to each lad and lass,
"Oh, boo worry! Shoo in a hurry!
Go off now and sweep! Sing those bugs to sleep!"

Perhaps comforting words came from a parent.

Night, Night, Tight

Night, night, tight.
Don't let the bed bugs bite.
The little child wails, "I don't have bugs!"
The parent hails, "Then watch the thugs!"

"Thugs? What do you mean?"
As the child laughs, amused,
The parent responds, "I'll tell you.
You need not be confused."

A thug at night is a notion
That robs you from your sleep.
Thugs visit your thoughts
And steal your peace and creep.

Thugs penetrate and keep you up at night,
Toss and turn with fear.
Your dreams may turn to fright.

Those thugs are like your worries.
You wish to fret no more,
Especially at nighttime.
A healthy spirit prays to restore.

"Don't let the thugs enter your mind,"
The parent said with hugs.
The child proclaims, "I don't want thugs!
I'll squash them, just like the bugs!"

Night, night, tight.
Don't let the bed thugs bite!

In the spirit of being tucked in at night as a child, wasn't it nice to be read a story at bedtime? The next few poems are poetic stories, all focusing on times of hurt and obscurity. Read them carefully to see what take-away message you receive. Remember, we all perceive differently.

Ice Cream Headaches and Brain Knots

The little girl approached her mother,
Teary eyed and sad with dismay.
Mother said, "Oh dear, Sally,
What's got you down today?"
Sally proclaimed, "I'm allergic
To vanilla, chocolate, and strawberry.
Ice cream gives me headaches.
Now I'm blue as a blueberry."
Her mother chuckled and calmly said,
"Ice cream, you need not refrain.
You're just having brain freeze,
And the cold sent messages to your brain."
Sally beamed with the biggest smile,
For she loves her ice cream and sicle pop.
She accepted Mother's words and then asked,
"Well, what messages will hot drop?"

Mother chuckled one more time
And then intently said,
"Hot will give you brain strain
As messages churn about in your head.
Mixed messages that feel spicy
Thought about over and over,
Not searing like heat bearing down,
But Sally, the story is not over.
Brain strain can last a very long time
Unlike momentary brain freeze.
It doesn't easily come and go
Like the winds and gentle breeze.
What we think can wear us down,
So focus on good thoughts.
Train your brain against the strain.
Counter friction to avoid brain knots.
Let your life counter friction.
Sally, learn this lesson today:
When hot feels like a clash of wills,
Tell that brain strain to go away!"

Hurry Up and Wait

They told the crowded room,
"Hurry up and wait."
We sat like clock watchers,
Thinking about destined fate.

I must have eyed the clock,
Minute by minute passing,
A long day of my life
Slipping by and passing.

There are things I'd rather do.
There are places I'd rather be.
It's not an overstretch to ask,
"Can't I take some time for me?"

As the seconds and minutes pass,
And the room is overly bored,
Is anyone else thinking of ships
And long planks to jump overboard?
Oh, if I could swim away
And not hurry up and wait,
I'd be propelling forward
And closer to home's gate.

Barely ten minutes have passed
Since I started this rhyme.
I guess I need to think about
God's time as perfect time.
Right on time, not early or late.
Is that what our maker would say?
It's only five minutes later.
Can the clock be wrong this day?

Hurry up and wait.
Slow down and be still.
It's a long test of patience,
A day to battle one's will.

And yes, I've heard it many times:
"All good things come to those who wait."
The clock doesn't stop ticking,
But God promises He'll give great!

The Symphony You Live

One ponders this. One ponders that,
The frivolous and the silly,
Filling his or her mind with random facts,
Watching time go by willy-nilly.

The one we'd call an enthusiast,
A deeply knowledgeable buff;
Holding passion for a special interest
Is good and well enough.

We each dance in our own rhythm,
How we hear our symphony.
Time is a gift from God.
Time is fleeting for you and me.

Temporal time on earth passes quickly,
So cherish every moment you live.
If frivolous doesn't feel right for you,
Then trust what you misgive.

If being an overly devoted fan
To sports, TV, the arts, and more
Isn't fit to your very likings,
Then change your life for sure.

Simply don't just doze off,
Nor watch the time go by.
The hands on the clock move slowly,
Almost naked to the eye.

But what you need to clearly see
Is how you live your days.
Don't live with personal illusions
But be happy with your ways.

What Goes Down Must Go Up

This morning I fell.
Tonight I rise.
Gazing at bright stars,
I commune under the skies.
My fall was bad, walked out of my shoes.
But tonight I walk, sharing good news.

I went through my day, thinking about gravity—
What goes up, must come down.
Gravity does not work the other way
If we were to say it the other way around.

What can go down and then go up,
I share in a spiritual defense:
Our attitudes, hopes, trust, and faith,
And all that makes up emotional sense.

Our seventh sense, these enlightened feelings,
Can't be measured like gravitational force.
But when we're feeling moody and sad,
We can let time run its course.
Troubles may bubble up and burst in due time,
So one can say the troubles came down.
But the direction for enlightened feelings
Needs to spin the other way around.

When you fall, you don't sit still.
You rise up off your butt.
It may hurt for a little while,
I say with an important "but."

And that *but* is to challenge you to say,
"What goes down must go up,"
And understand we're speaking of
The emotions you pour in your cup.

For if you're pouring hopelessness,
Then that is what you will drink.
If you're pouring faith and hope,
Your emotions will follow your think.
Think up and drink up.
What goes down must go up.

Colorful Emotions

Tough to end the year.
Rough to start a new.
If color holds emotions,
Would all the months be blue?

January, white as snow,
The forerunner of the calendar show.

February pink,
A paler form of red.
Many heartfelt unions
As Valentine's lovers move ahead.

Green and lush lands blossom,
As March, April, May so bring.
Celebrate warmth and new life,
The wonderful season of spring.

June, the passionate wedding month,
Unions sealed with a kiss.
Red be the color of love
With dreams for lifelong bliss.

What happens now over the half point?
July's unclear to me.
The seventh month of the year
Might be black as mystery.
The same could be said for any month,
For each and every day follows another.
We really can't be sure what any day will bring
Or match to any clear color.

One thing is common about August.
The sun shines yellow and hot.
A warm time may be a story,
The uncertainties we haven't forgot.

Orange and brown lands fade
In September, October, and November.
Honor coolness and passing life,
The season of fall we remember.

December is strung about
With tinsel of silver and gold.
Another year has passed,
So what have the colors told?

Seasons change. Questions arise.
With certainty, we generalize.
Matching colors to what we see.
The seasons will be as they will be.
The seasons dealt what they have dealt,
Perhaps by colors we have felt.

See Red, Feel Blue, Pause ... Then Go

If life were monitored by a traffic light,
When hurting we'd see red,
Warning us to simply stop
And welcome grace ahead.
When seeking knowledge and change,
We'd see yellow as time-out,
A pausing state of reflection
And time to alter what we doubt.
When we are ready to dawn
And act with a fresh start,
We'd decidedly see the green light,
So lustrous and set apart.

For in those times everybody hurts,
Blue describes our woeful hearts.
The blue of pain, the yellow of pause,
Urges us forth to make new starts.
Moving forward is a readiness time
Following penetration of red, yellow, and blue.
Though we don't physically see these colors
Along with green, they propel us to feel new.
If the traffic light stops blinking,
Your inner light still shines,
With hope and faith and trust
Beyond the lights of power lines.
So let God be your power,
Your traffic light per se,
The ultimate guider and perfect light
To steer you on your way.

The Disparity of Being Green

Everybody hurts,
But everything is fine.
Goodness will be restored
By His ever-loving vine;
That far reaches and touches
Everyone who brings
Good from the branches from which we hang.
We are fruit that clings.

When it feels like everything hurts,
Trust everyone is fine.
You will feel good again
And not feel woeful and pine.

In times of pine, think evergreen,
The greenest tree that you have seen,
Retaining green leaves through the year,
But seems there's a disparity to note and clear.

For if you think evergreen
Means green forever sure,
Green in other terms
Defines unripe and immature.

Green is the color of balance,
Equilibrium between head and heart.
But like a young, scantly green sapling,
We were little sprout babies from the start.

I guess you can say we all were green,
Maturing to acquire the nurturance of green,
A state of harmony and growth,
Relaxed by head and heart—yes, both.
Evergreen.
Ever green?
Most stately tree
I've ever seen.

Let's not forget that animals hurt too; those in the wild fight to survive. Those that are neglected want to be protected.

The Doe Cries to the Leopard

I am dying day by day,
Just a slow and rotting decay.
Limp as if I have no blood,
A walking carcass in a flood.

A flood that churns
As each day turns.
A flood that bites
With pains and frights.

A flood that may not knock me off my feet
But one that lashes with each heart's beat.
So as you watch my carcass of bones,
I feel you stare at my statue of stones.

You even proclaim, "I hope you die!"
The carcass ashes may float to the sky,
As if to plan your next attack
With lurking eyes behind my back.

For the bloodless carcass surely knows
She's hunted like prey wherever she goes.
When comes the day, the final hour,
The predator makes good on his final devour?

Say what you mean and mean what you say,
Else all we are are predator and prey.

We see changes in nature as time passes.

The Wreath Withers

The wreath of pine and holly berries,
Which hung in red, white, and green,
Is lackluster with no blossom,
No longer brightly seen.

Can't nourish with water to drink nor sugar to eat.
The berries are shriveled and now dried.
The needles not fallen are brown and withered,
Now fallen to the ground at the side.

The Unclothed Dandelion

A dandelion I once saw in full bloom
Prominently stood against the countryside's room.

Alone, unprotected, in a vast field
With very few wispies,
Nothing left to shield.

For the wind swept those elements of its age
Into the air to simply disengage.

Soon it will be just a naked stem,
Disconnected from the life it once had,
When a field of yellow clothed the countryside,
And now that room's barely clad.

We have witnessed and recall scary and raging natural disasters.

The Storm Raged

The night the perfect storm was in rage,
The landscape shook on a dramatic stage.

Others watched in sorrow,
Crying, "Let there be a tomorrow!"
We watched our brothers and sisters
Face horrid weather-torn twisters.

A torrential shower disrupted power.
Towns and cities went dark.
Shrill screams were frightening.
Blazing flames arose from the spark.

A hurricane, deemed a superstorm,
United forces in nature together;
Bonded to wreak havoc,
Produced titanic stormy weather.

Storms of wrath
Hit every known path,
Trapping those who tried to flee,
Dropping bodies to bended knee.

The souls cried. This great divide—
Wind, fire, and rain—acted in rage.
The storms of anger stole the stage.

We have witnessed the tragedies and losses experienced through times of war.

In Wars of Death

As fellowship crumbles,
The affiliation tumbles.
We all fall to the ground.

Stripped and defenseless,
We seem so senseless.
We all lie on the ground.

The ground feels like a burial site,
Where we grasped our last breath.
Plagued and overcome we are
By such maddening wars of death.

Loved ones pass on. Circumstances lead some we love to other paths meant for them. Yet for us, letting go is hard.

Good-bye

Sometimes when I'm feeling blue,
I take a moment to reflect on you.
The words you say inspire me
To be all who I can be.

You've opened up your heart to share
Many thoughts that show you care.
You've listened with an open ear
To my sorrows, pain, and fear.

So now I shed my tears no more;
I see hope through an open door.
I keep on walking head held high.
It's so hard to say good-bye.

You'll always be a part of me.
You've helped to set me ever free.
Whether close or far away,
I'll think of you each passing day.

As time passes, we feel the pangs of an empty nest. As we age, we look back at earlier chapters of our lives, and we reflect. We want to be remembered, and having many chances to bond closely with others is important. We realize life on Earth is short. It is finite.

Beyond Barbie and Cartoon Icons

Some days her body feels
Like all limbs could be ripped off,
Like a Barbie doll held in a little girl's hand,
Whose dressy clothes she'll put on and doff.

Barbie's limbs could be removed,
As she is just a doll,
But a doll the little girl treasures
As most beautiful of her dolls in all.

On those saddening fall-apart days,
It's true strength to not give up,
When everyone else may not understand,
Who commune with her close up.

For sometimes she retreats,
Just thinking about Barbie's dream house
Or simply living in a cartoon world
Of Mickey and Minnie Mouse.

Living in an imaginary world
Of toys lavished with attention.
But then one day the children grow up,
And she's left with apprehension.

Feeling the pangs of an empty nest,
The anxiety and loneliness,
As her arms seem to be disjointing
From her upper-body chest.

She craves to extend her arms
And feel her legs in motion
And not feel so inanimate,
Like Barbie without emotion.

Barbie is so beautiful,
But in her older age,
The once-young girl herself
Drifts back to an olden page.

Like pages in a storybook,
Reading what comes next:
Once-upon-a-time openings
And living-happily-ever text.

Barbie's like an icon now,
Living on year by year
In her world of plastic,
Which has no single fear.

For if she's unattended to,
Like fads quickly here and gone,
The girl who lives in this story
Wants to be remembered as life goes on.

Sometimes we long for a second chance with someone we lost contact with in an earlier time. Sometimes, we really do get those second chances!

Second Chance

A long time ago.
Confused by friend or foe?
Over real or fake,
Not knowing what to make
Of words and actions, heard and seen.
Was there distorted meaning in between?

Did I see right through you?
Perhaps I never knew you.
Or not quite well enough
To hang in there quite tough.

I saw your form and shadow,
Maybe not enough more.
Now in a later time in life,
Let's see what we missed before.

Likewise on your end.
Confused by foe or friend?
Thinking just like I,
Was it truth or lie?

Regardless of the happenings of first chance,
Opportunity knocks beyond circumstance,
As if there always was a bond,
Of which we once were very fond.

If second chance means a better friend,
A bond sealed to last always,
Then friendship must be the right union
To last us all our days.

Yet despite life's challenges, we recall God's beautiful rainbow in the sky. It reminds us to seek and walk a bright, illuminated path to Him. Our eyes follow the colorful arc with hope and reliance on God's promises. We stare at the luminous stars shining over our heads. We are cheerful and thankful that God created rainbows and stars.

Promise

Starlight,
Star bright.
Let me make a wish this night.

Shine so bright.
Never grow dim.
Illuminate
The path to Him.

When holding and carrying on are hard,
Heal those wounds where all have scarred.

When lonely nights
We're teary eyed
And cannot count
Teardrops we've cried.

Penetrate light
Beyond our skin,
Promising us
We can invincibly win.

We want to lean on the Lord's shoulders and be held in everlasting arms. We want to get beyond uttering cries of "Why me?" and "Why now?" and "If only."

The Lord's Shoulders

Live hope in trying times.
Seek intimacy on the Lord's shoulder.
Living personal agony, we all know,
Could make us feel much colder.
When you start to feel indifferent,
Unfriendly, and maybe frigid,
Distant, aloof, and reserved,
And your days have grown so rigid.
But you can bend, and you can change.
Be positive to what the Lord will arrange.
Lean on His shoulders when you feel stiff
With wrong attitudes and questions with "if,"
For all those ifs and wonder whys
Are the Lord's concerns for Him to reply.
So tap at His door, even each shoulder.
He'll answer your deep personal cry.

To get to a better place with yourself and others, sometimes we must let ourselves feel the cries of Jesus and how we would feel if nails wounded us.

Cracked by Wood

Pains from feelings that are mine
As I cling to God, our vine.
Hanging on a cross of wood,
Seeking out the common good.
I'm a branch, and you are too.
What has happened to our view?
To first love God with all your heart;
That is commanded from the start.
Then, as Jesus so loved you,
Love one another, be so true.
And not feel bound and nailed to wood
From wounded hearts meant to do good.
Jesus drew His final breath
From a heart of divine depth.
Let your hearts not feel attacked
But filled with love where they've so cracked.

The best part of all is that we act, and we go to our Father's feet. We kneel and pray. Whatever hurts or concerns we have, we offer them up to our Father, as we have so much to say.

Father, Take Thy Cup

Some see the cup half empty,
While others see it half full.
Are you one of those tempted persons
Who feels pressured by drag and pull?

When you focus on your worries,
You create more fret, not less.
The sheer weight of fret alone
Will cause your soul to digress.

You'd like to fill the cup and your life
Up to its very rim,
Even wishing for an overflow
In a preference to be full, not slim.

Or maybe you've packed your life so tight,
Like brown sugar smashed with a spoon,
That you feel no breathing room,
And you'll burst like an over-inflated balloon.

Either way you describe it,
Anxiety is consuming you.
So drink from a cup of blessings
To realize God is seeking you.

You'll start to see *fill* and *fulfill* are really not the same
And that you have been spinning around in quite an endless game.
So cast your emptiness and tightness to the One who is truly endless.
God is infinity and beyond. He created His world so tremendous.

Our Father will take any cup,
Your cup and all you have to bear.
He will never deny your reach and stretch
But return comfort beyond compare.

"Father, take thy cup
That I offer today.
Hear these very words
As I kneel and pray."

Be Still

With Father   Son   Holy Spirit

Be Still and Know

Know more by being still. That may sound a bit inactive as an approach. However, in this section I invite you to pause. Be still. Come to realize how productive being still can be.

Know has multiple meanings. In one sense, to know is to become aware. In another sense, to know is to develop familiarity and relationships with others.

In this section, I emphasize both to allow you to become conscious of and realize important lessons and principles to carry forward and act with greater purpose and fulfillment. I also invite you to strengthen your relationships with God, Jesus, yourself, and others.

This section not only is spiritually based but also stresses wellness emotionally, mentally, and physically. We are all multifaceted individuals. There are other forms of wellness, such as social, environmental, and occupational; and it is very important that we be well-balanced individuals. We drive toward peace, harmony, and quality of life.

In the first section, I threaded poetry together by introductory captions. I hope you read and noticed the "hurt" section as one large story in and of itself.

In this section, I invite you to listen to the voice of God for guidance and your own inner voice for intuition.

A Wondrous Story

Lord, let me use a gift of writing
To speak Your name in glory,
To honor and to tribute,
To tell a wondrous story.

We all have our own stories, which God helps to write and paint.

Master, Master

God, be our masterpiece.
Paint our stories piece by piece.
God, be our master peace.
Light our lives with love and peace.

Personally for me, writing this memoir has been fulfilling and inspirational. You could say that my "one day dawned" with its completion. My own dreams materialized before my eyes in black and white.

One Day

One day when it's time,
Let there be
A servant position, fulfilling for me.

Beyond the rat race,
Beyond the text,
To glorify "Father,"
A step that is next.

For years I've written
In spiritual rhyme,
My life on paper
A memoir in time.

I've written the dark,
Then turned words to light;
David and Psalms
Made landscape so bright.

For the biblical heroes,
Remind me all falter.
When I'm hard on myself,
I must turn to the psalter.

God forgives me when
I don't do the same,
When I feel humiliated
Or sometimes feel shame.

One day He makes us more sensitive,
More freely to thank and foremost forgive.
If every day were just like "one day,"
Each step we take would be sunny, not gray.

But it takes gray steps,
Where white and black blend,
To find inner peace
And be your own friend.

I invite you to journey with me and start to see things differently. You may even desire to be a poet of light.

Cast Your Eyes

If I were a painter of light,
I'd paint with strokes of hope.
If I were a poet of light,
I'd inspire with words to cope.

Creating stories and impressions
To overcome our human transgressions.

Blotting out hateful ways of thinking,
Soaring without look-away blinking.

For writing resembles a painting,
Expressions cast in art.
It only takes a spark,
And imagination will soon start.

The audience's reaction is next,
Interpretation of the text.

Reading once, reading twice
Over and over could be nice.

Seeing what you hadn't before,
Brighter light upon your shore.

Whatever form of art,
Cast your eyes repeatedly.
It's your freedom to interpret
And see things differently.

My idea for this section of the memoir came from my Bible cover. My Bible cover is black and white. The upper portion has a white background with black flowers. The lower portion has a black background with white flowers. In the middle, the following Bible verse is printed:

Be still and know that I am God! Psalm 46:10

This is one of my favorite verses. My Bible is the one I received as a youth at the completion of confirmation class and upon joining my hometown church. It pleases me to have carried around this same Bible all these years.

It is not my goal to theologically train you. However, I hope I instill a desire for you to reach out and regularly read the Bible. Forge a deeper relationship with God.

Throughout this section, I have included Bible verses that have special meaning to me and help to support the messages I'm conveying through the poetry.

Let's begin with "Be Still and Know God."

God is our infinity and beyond. Everything. He is our all. We can describe Him in so many ways. Yet in a sense, He is also indescribable as if so complex beyond our understanding. He is the very reason we have a Bible. God gave words so others could author the Bible.

Second Timothy 3:16 says, "All Scripture is God-breathed and is useful for teaching, rebuking, correcting and training in righteousness."

Guided by One, Two, and Three

One large promise of promises:
Two testaments, old and new.
The Trinity of three speaking
The "truths" for sheep to turn to.
For aren't we all but sheep,
Seeking membership in a herd?
Shepherded by our Lord
And guided by holy Word.
Children of God so seeking
A bond that will never die.
To not feel bound in shackles and chains
But free from dark and lie.
Fellowship walking in the light,
Away from darkness and plight.
One large book of promises
For sheep to follow forthright.

God gave us destiny.

First Corinthians 2:9 says, "However, as it is written: 'What no eye has seen, what no ear has heard, and what no human mind has conceived'—the things God has prepared for those who love him."

A Word Called Destiny

We learn as little children
What defines a noun.
A person, place, or thing,
Not at all profound.

Let's look a little deeper
At a word called "destiny."
A who? A where? A what?
What definition shall it be?

If you believe a who,
Would you then say God?
Or perhaps His Son at His side,
Jesus's footsteps, can we trod?

If you search for a place,
Is it heaven you would say?
A place of ideal and perfection,
A garden where sin's been washed away?

If you seek a thing
In the Bible, will you find?
The Word, good news, a Book of Life;
A guiding message to renew the mind.

Put them all together,
Find meaning called a purpose;
A comfortable, fulfilling sense.
God, heaven, and Bible transform us.

We need "destiny" to teach us
Just how to live on Earth.
The Bible teaches us spiritual growth
Till we meet God and experience rebirth.

Isaiah 40:8 says, "The grass withers and the flowers fall, but the word of our God endures forever."

Imagine God whispering to you now in a still, small voice.

Journey Together

You may not understand Me,
But I am not your enemy.

You may want something otherwise,
But trust My promises are not lies.

Your future is in My hands,
So with confidence you must walk.
But never be afraid to seek Me;
I want your time and talk.

I delight when you kneel and pray.
I'm open every single day
To know and hear your thoughts
Directly as you speak.
For whether you whisper or shout,
You are strong, not weak.

Come to Me for any reason.
Come to Me in any season.

When you feel
Happy and stable
Or when you feel
Sad and unable.

To know where to quite turn next,
I'll help you with your steps.
United we will journey together
To bottomless, spiritual depths.

He whispers, "I am by your side."

Romans 8:31 says, "What, then, shall we say in response to these things? If God is for us, who can be against us?"

Be

Don't shy away; you can't hide.
I'm right here by your side.
I'm your God; I so speak.
We're not playing hide-and-seek.
As you close your eyes and count to ten,
I do not run like small children.
Never doubt this on an insecure day;
That day will pass, so come My way.
Instead I ask that you seek Me.
I'll never hide or let you be.
As you open your eyes, ready to see,
You'll feel me here; I am. I be.

He whispers, "I am Father. You are My children."

Galatians 3:26 says, "So in Christ Jesus you are all children of God through faith."

Children of God

God didn't call us to be lone rangers,
Nor unsociable, disregarding strangers.
He does want us to protect each other,
Averting the harms of rebellions and dangers.
God didn't call us to be superheroes,
But He does want us to be strong.
We don't possess supernatural powers,
But we are strong when we get along.
God didn't call us to be shiny knights,
Rescuing all those in distress.
But He does want us to deeply care,
Be affectionate to others, and bless.
God calls us to be chosen, set apart,
Holy, faithful, and pure in heart.
God didn't call us to be wanderers,
Dwelling in the Land of Nod.
Very importantly, He calls us to make peace,
And we will be called "children of God."

He whispers, "I am Creator of the universe."

Genesis 1:1 says, "In the beginning God created the heavens and the earth."

All That God Has Made

Look all around everywhere.
Everything God has made.
The world is a vast spectrum
Of every color and shade.

Even more than the rainbow
Made up of ROYGBIV
Seven beautiful colors,
Reminding us how to live.

Red, orange, yellow;
Warm ones on the outside.
Green, blue, indigo, and violet;
Cool fills the arc on the inside.

If a rainbow shone permanently as a sign in the sky,
Would we live more hopefully by those colors we eye?

Momentary flashes of the ROYGBIV arc fade,
But look around everywhere
For all that God has made.

He whispers, "My creations are good."

Genesis 1:31 says, "God saw all that he had made, and it was very good. And there was evening, and there was morning—the sixth day."

The Goodness of God's Creations

May you soar like an eagle with mighty wings
Over a flowing ocean, with a song it so sings.

For the water speaks with whispers and roars,
Echoing melodies as it reaches the shores.

Harmonies, each sea billow swells.
Are you listening to the story one tells?

Until the next one rolls in for its landing
And wakens your senses to deep understanding.

Messages that reflect up high to the skies,
Where the eagles are so very wise.

Closer they be to our majestic heaven;
God also made earth, then rested on seven.

In just six days, His creation was done.
He created it all and the light of the sun,

Divided time into day and night,
Gave us wonders, gave man sight.

He declared the goodness of all,
Creations so vast, wide, and so tall.

He whispers, "I created birds and desire you to soar spiritually. Soar like an eagle!"

Isaiah 40:31 says, "But those who hope in the Lord will renew their strength. They will soar on wings like eagles. They will run and not grow weary. They will walk and not be faint."

Where Birds Do Fly

Speak to me, Lord;
I'll write thoughts of You,
However mysterious,
As I look yonder blue.

The sky is Your vastness
So eternally high,
Far, far beyond
Where the birds do fly.

Yet like a bird, I can compare;
Your will and freedom soar in the air.

Like a majestic cardinal
Or a peaceful, white dove,
Like a mighty eagle
Sent to teach us to love.

Like a wise owl,
Seeing clearly at night,
Dear Lord, fill the darkness
And cast holy light.

He whispers, "I make the wind blow. Feel its freshness on your face."

John 3:8 says, "The wind blows wherever it pleases. You hear its sound, but you cannot tell where it comes from or where it is going. So it is with everyone born of the Spirit."

Feel the Wind

I welcome the quiet,
Such a comforting hush.
No hustle, no bustle.
I'm not in a rush.

With quiet brings patience;
Tranquility flows.
The Spirit extols
As wind softly blows.

The wind carries messages,
Beautiful lessons to learn.
Feel the wind on your face.
Let God's Spirit churn.

Feel the wind
When not a sound does it make,
Or when it's tumultuous
And thrusts with loud shake.

The wind is God's,
His creation alone.
It quiets my soul
With harmonious tone.

He whispers, "I color the sky with rainbows. See hope in their beauty."

Genesis 9:13 says, "I have set my rainbow in the clouds, and it will be the sign of the covenant between me and the earth."

Rainbow of Hope

If a rainbow were permanently in the sky,
No floods to ever wash good-bye.

Would we spend each day feeling more secure?
Face each day with more courage and endure—
The times when things feel hard and trying;
Complications overt; whatever's underlying.

Issues apparent that conceal otherwise.
Issues ambiguous, much like a disguise.

The rainbow is a covenant of hope.
No flood will ever destroy all flesh.
We only see it a few times a year,
Yet daily, God's here for refresh.

A freshening outlook, a refreshed hope
That every day is a fresh start,
Arching from the arc of God,
Who shines beauty within each heart.

He whispers "I am the vine."

John 15:5 says, "I am the vine; you are the branches. If you remain in me and I in you, you will bear much fruit; apart from me you can do nothing."

Tree of Life

You are a Tree of Life
Counting on me
To speak of glory
From the vine You so be.

Knowing some branches
Will survive the storms,
Not break apart
But choose to reform.

For every branch sins and errs in its ways.
But when vine lives in branch, we're bonded all days.

The life of Your vine,
So spiritually divine,
Nourishes and reforms
As branches face storms.

So counsel and feed me
From vine to branch.
Count on me
In all circumstance.

He whispers, "Listen. Come to Me in prayer."

Philippians 4:6 says, "Do not be anxious about anything, but in every situation, by prayer and petition, with thanksgiving, present your requests to God."

Surrender

Spirit, take me as I am,
My conflicts, tension, and worry.
Revolutionize my soul;
Tomorrow is a new story.

To live beyond my circumstances,
Believing and taking chances,
Even in the bleakest hour
I am anxious with no power.

I must not try to usurp more,
When I rightfully must surrender
An action that's not giving up
But accepting God's will so tender.

For His will may prove me wrong,
For He is always right.
He always knows the best for me.
I surrender to His might.

He calls for you to relinquish control and roll with His flow.

Roll with the Flow

If only I could grasp tomorrow,
Make sense of days thereafter;
Hold tomorrow in my hand,
Replace the tears with laughter.
For what I do not comprehend,
I may try to control.
Oh, dear Lord, let me step back,
And let Your flow so roll,
For You are the pinnacle,
I cannot rise above.
But I can step inside myself
And find Your guiding love.

Be still and listen to His call.

Isaiah 30:21 says, "Whether you turn to the right or to the left, your ears will hear a voice behind you, saying, 'This is the way; walk in it.'"

Tall and Firm

Are you not getting anywhere?
Feel free to stop in your tracks.
Lose your mobility for a moment.
Stand still and just relax.

Standing still is not human nature.
We want to constantly move.
Maybe we simply don't realize
By being "still," we can really improve.

To stand tall is standing firm.
To stand firm is standing tall.
Adopt a new, strong posture
And listen for God's call.
Then, when you clearly hear it,
Put your feet forward in a new stride.
Discernment takes ahold of you,
Prepares your heart bona fide.

Be still and know He is a defender.

Psalm 91: 14–15 says, "'Because he loves me,' says the Lord, 'I will rescue him; I will protect him, for he acknowledges my name. He will call on me, and I will answer him; I will be with him in trouble, I will deliver him and honor him.'"

Through Any Storm

I've worked hard, paid my dues,
Walked this life in many shoes.
Held your hand; you held mine
In times when things were not so fine.
Shared gratitude, sympathies, and grace,
Smiles and hugs with loving embrace.
Seized moments, experienced thrills.
Felt goose bumps during scary chills.
But one thing can keep me warm,
Is steadfast love through any storm.

Be still and know He is divine intervention. He protects us from being snared by those with false intentions.

Second Samuel 22:3 says, "My God is my rock, in whom I take refuge, my shield and the horn of my salvation. He is my stronghold, my refuge and my savior—from violent people you save me."

Wise to the Serpent

Servant kneeling in the house of prayer,
Be wise and ever aware
Of false prophets and serpents,
Who deceive and aim to snare.

Hear God's voice above those clothed
And robed with false intentions;
Be discerning to those you meet
And trust in divine interventions.

God has your back
As you look ahead.
He is your protective rock
In this earthly homestead.

God is a refuge,
A shield and a stronghold;
He is wise to the serpents
Who twisted what they told.

Be still and know He is a friend to those who fear Him.

Psalm 25:14 says, "The Lord confides in those who fear him; he makes his covenant known to them."

Drifting

Dark colors I've experienced
Show me I need light
For common everyday experiences
That have left me so uptight.

Light shining like the Twenty-third Psalm,
Leads me where I can be calm;
Beside still waters to fill my cup,
To runneth over as I face up;
To my fear of You, oh Lord,
For Your very name's sake;
In a deep, lush valley,
Threatened by no snake.

Lord, You walk with me.
My fear of You is a gift.
I will fear no evil.
You carry me like a drift.

Like downstream currents of water or air,
Moving me as the currents flow …
Toward a path of righteousness
That You want me to know.

You want me to follow You
All the days of my life;
To realize that I shall not want,
Lord, shepherd me from strife.

Be still and know He protects us when we seek sanctuary.

Psalm 4:8 says, "In peace I will lie down and sleep, for you alone, Lord, make me dwell in safety."

Seeking Sanctuary

We see no visible footprints.
We can't smell his scent.
We are warned as God's followers
Of the disguised angel, who is bent,
Crooked like a slithering snake,
Hidden in tall grass,
Camouflaged, and on the prowl;
We seek a path to surpass—

The Devil's temptations we do call sin,
God has our back to help us win;
Especially when we feel so frail,
God knows the Devil follows our trail.

Like a serpent, lion, or wolf,
Who lurks to snatch God's sheep;
We followers seek the sanctuary of God,
And the protection of our souls, Abba keep.

We are all responsible for our actions
And can't use Satan as a scapegoat.
We are commanded to love our Lord and neighbors,
And to follow what the Bible does quote.

Be still and know He is a provider.

Psalm 145:14 says, "The Lord upholds all who fall and lifts up all who are bowed down."

He Decides

If you're like me,
It's hard to say,
"It's all good.
Come what may."
Take it as it comes,
What He provides,
To satisfy needs
As He decides.

Accept what He gives
As He shapes you
To grow at a pace
Authentically true.
God will take care
Of you and me
With spiritual renewal
That's gentle and free.

Be still and know He has plans for everyone.

Jeremiah 29:11 says, "'For I know the plans I have for you,' declares the Lord, 'plans to prosper you and not to harm you, plans to give you hope and a future.'"

Ahead of Any Mystery

Be still and know.
I'm right where I need to be.
A master plan's unfolding
That only God can see.
Maybe I have frustrations
When the plan is not going my way.
Maybe I have temptations
And want to change the course of the day.
Whatever each day has brought me,
It happened for a reason.
What lies ahead any mystery today,
God will reveal each season.

Have patience and confidence in God's works and plans to fulfill your heart's desires.

Psalm 37:4 says, "Take delight in the Lord, and he will give you the desires of your heart."

Desire So Stitched

Life is good,
Works out as it should
By God's master plan
For each woman and man.

We live day by day,
Paving our very way,
Not knowing what's around the bend,
What new message He will send;
So that spiritual growth is enriched,
So that desire becomes so stitched.
Like threads, like veins, that run to the heart,
Intaking the glory God has to impart.

Especially in times of anxiousness, God's works will feel like a mystery.

Job 12:22 says, "He reveals the deep things of darkness and brings utter darkness into the light."

Mighty Works

Little one, not yet grown up,
Held in the palm of God's hand.
Aren't you just the anxious one
To learn what God has planned?

Sometimes He closes His hand,
And then you cannot see
The mighty works He's doing,
A big picture that will one day be.

Then in God's own time,
He opens His hand ever wide
Beyond the once-invisible scenes;
His mighty works are bona fide.

God leads us to the mysterious wilderness, a landscape filled with trails to choose.

Deuteronomy 8:2 says, "Remember how the Lord your God led you all the way in the wilderness these forty years, to humble and test you in order to know what was in your heart, whether or not you would keep his commands."

Reasons and Surprises

Everything happens for a reason.
I believe this to be true.
A mighty plan is being worked out,
Though disguised from me and you.

At the perfect time, the master plan unveils,
Unfolding like a drape;
Neatly hung before your eyes,
Arranged like an artist's landscape.

The landscape blends the scenery
With every speck in place.
God's master plan, once puzzling,
Is complete with every trace.

I think about those wandering footsteps
Blazing through the wilderness trails.
Yes, life is like steps in the wilderness,
Learning about survival and details.

Such growth may seem mysterious
Like divisions in our lives.
We never see a curtain
That carefully falls, nor does it rise.

We blaze through the wilderness
With no cameras and no light.
The wilderness is not a fancy stage
Where we act and are cued on sight.

Through childhood, adolescence, adulthood,
We experience many falls and rises;
But God allows those happenings
To be for reasons and surprises.

Be still and know that each day is one day at a time.

Matthew 6:34 says, "Therefore do not worry about tomorrow, for tomorrow will worry about itself. Each day has enough trouble of its own."

No Tomorrow Today

The tomorrow we know as the unknown,
He who sits upon the throne
Knows and doesn't share.
The future He won't bare.

That's what makes the present
The day before tomorrow.
Today you know yesterday's unknown,
But tomorrow you can't borrow.

Trust in God's timing.

Ecclesiastes 3:1 says, "There is a time for everything, and a season for every activity under the heavens."

Right on Time

Wait on the Lord
When your strength is depleted.
Trust in His timing.
Do not feel defeated.

Gods knows His plans for you.
Everything is right on time.
Gods knows His plans for me.
His clock has perfect chime.

The very day called "today" may bring such unexpected favor.

Proverbs 27:1 says, "Do not boast about tomorrow, for you do not know what a day may bring."

Now

To honor that wonderful moment called "now,"
Expectancy, favor, planned by Him; that's how.
Expectancy, the long-awaited favor,
Granted to you, yours to savor.
As you showed honor and longed for a break,
A gloryful chance, timed just right, now to take.
Envision what God may do for you;
He protects, He delivers, and He sees your way through.

Imagine possibilities, but do not try to predict the future. There are no glass objects like mirrors and crystal balls that give us such vision. Cast aside your anxieties and fears.

Ecclesiastes 7:14 says, "When times are good, be happy; but when times are bad, consider this: God has made the one as well as the other. Therefore, no one can discover anything about their future."

No Looking Glass

Oh wounded one,
You little lad,
A son of God,
Don't be so sad.
Oh wounded soul,
You little lass,
A daughter of God,
Your woe will pass.
Cheer up, children;
Don't be afraid.
Remember Jesus
And the price He paid.
Don't worry so;
Let your life unfold.
In times of woe,
Be brave and bold.
God will prosper you, lad and lass,
In the absence of mirrors,
No looking glass.

Be still and know He is a pivot. He can turn things around.

Job 37:12 says, "At his direction [the clouds] swirl around over the face of the whole earth to do whatever he commands them."

His All

No pain, no gain.
Come sun, come rain.
Look up, look down.
Some smile, some frown.
Look left, look right.
Some dim, some bright.
Moods shift, spirits lift.
Emotions shake, feelings wake.

Fires burn, tides turn.
The active flames once came,
Yielding a mighty message:
Extinguish the present-day "same."

Change offers discovery points
From our old turning joints,
Where we seek to pivot
From such a tiny rivet.

Seated on a tiny pin,
We could so easily fall,
But when God is our pivot,
We oscillate for His all.

Be still and know He can give you new dreams and visions.

Ephesians 3:20 says, "Now to him who is able to do immeasurably more than all we ask or imagine, according to his power that is at work within us."

Dream On

When a vision is all it turns out to be
And the dream didn't turn into reality
And we fold our hands like a deck of cards
And accept it's time the fantasy retards,
We're reminded it's okay to dream.
It's a natural thing to do.
Some future day, a new dream
Will turn out so vividly true.

Be still and know He can turn messes into messages.

Philippians 3:21 says, "Who, by the power that enables him to bring everything under his control, will transform our lowly bodies so that they will be like his glorious body."

Glorious Mess

Be happy and blessed,
Calm and not stressed.

Careful with tongue,
Playful and young.

Get down on your knees.
Say, "Thank you" and "Please."

To your ever-present witness
Who takes care of your fitness

In more ways than one,
So don't fear and run

In the direction away
He wants you to stay.

He wants you to seek,
Be humble and meek.

He promises devotion
In return for your emotion.

God wants your heart
From its pure start.

God wants your best
As you work and rest.

God wants your all
And nothing less.
He creates messages
From your glorious mess.

Be still and know He helps you shine. When we see His light, we transform and gleam.

Psalm 36:9 says, "For with you is the fountain of life; in your light we see light."

Shine and Gleam

Bigger than my fears,
Larger than my doubts,
Broader than my anxieties,
Wider than my pouts.

All knowing of my ins and outs,
All that makes me tick,
Comforter when I'm ill,
Healer when I'm sick.

There when I feel helpless,
Hearing every thought,
Witness to my insecurities and
Battles I have fought.

To make it to a better place
That holds tender peace and grace;
That boosts my very self-esteem
So like You, I shine and gleam.

Be still and know He is our Redeemer.

Psalm 19:14 says, "May these words of my mouth and this meditation of my heart be pleasing in your sight, Lord, my Rock and my Redeemer."

From Critic to Contented

Being your own worst critic
Equals judging yourself harshly.
Frustration mounts so paramount;
You feel contentment only partially.
Such a stance is not enduring.
It can sustain for just a brief time,
Until you're so uncomfortable,
As life feels like a draining climb.

Remind yourself of our Redeemer.
He is not criticizing you.
He wants to make you better,
For being a critic is not fit for you.
He wants you to see you're everything
Yet nothing without Him;
He wants you to discard faulty opinions of yourself
That you take on like a whim.

"Is contentment a secret?" so the critic does ask
As if he cries for help, staring through a half mask.
Having holes just for the eyes,
The critic parades through warped disguise.
For others who've found contentment,
Notice the critic wears a fake smile,
Facing inner torment
Behind the half mask worn in style.

If you are so hard on yourself and so preoccupied,
Learn to rest in God's providence, and He'll be glorified.
Our Redeemer has purpose, and He will make you see
You too have a unique purpose, like all men equally.
God chants, "Remember Me! Hold onto Me with reliance."
Being your own worst critic is just a form of wary defiance.
Be thankful when you have little
And say extra thanks when you have so much.
Look out for the interests of others,
The human lives you may deeply touch.

God cares. He reels us in when we swim too far.

Reeled In

Reel me in like a fish.
I'll gladly take the bait.
Return to God after time-out;
Surely I won't wait.

God so wants us steadily
To seek Him ever readily.
With Him time-out can be so long;
He loves us in our rights and wrongs.

When there's weeping desolation,
He'll be churning consolation;
Participating in our fights,
So we may graduate to new heights.
Be glad when you're caught and snared,
Reeled in tightly by His cares.

He draws us closer when we drift, freely taking us back each time we need connection.

Draw Me Closer

Draw me in like a magnet,
Closer, side by side.
When You feel me slipping away,
Pull me back to confide.

When I need to share
What's truly on my mind,
To not feel taut like a yo-yo
But comfortable to unwind.

When I'm drawn so close,
Hear my deep confessions;
Echo back in such a way
That I may learn Your lessons.

When You release me into
The great big world again,
Tell me I'm free to come back,
Like a magnet You pull in.

With God, you will not walk alone. A solitary walk may feel like the path of least resistance as you try to avoid turning your troubles over to God. Trust God to take care of you. Walk with God and stride "the path of most resistance" and reap the rewards of change and progress.

A Hard, Worthy Workout

Are you deciding to live with distance?
Striding along the path of least resistance?
The latter is phrased in question form,
For the trusting path may feel out of norm.
We tend to choose what's easiest
And avoid pain over doing better and right;
In this situation to minimize pain,
Your dearest support, you've so lost sight.
Spiritually, you may be resisting God
To walk along the more challenged pathway.
Then you may miss out on His best for you,
And so herein I choose to say:
We can't find a path without less pain
If we're constantly walking alone,
For God wants to work harder in your life
And reward you with the unknown.
All the rivers flow into the sea,
But this chosen path is a new one, you'll see.
Any wind blows in some path unknown;
Any path walked with God, you'll not walk alone.
Deciding to take "the path of most resistance"
Is an action of trust to go with God for the distance.
Choosing a path to shape your life even more
Will be a hard, worthy workout. I say this for sure.

Let God be your support so you may walk on solid ground.

My Walking Stick

The tender ground is shaky, where do I put my feet?
I cannot see clearly where the two ends meet.
Is there a chasm up ahead, not narrow but too wide?
If I can't cross it alone, then take me by Your side.
If that crossing gets too rough, won't You carry me?
Like one set of footprints in sand, below us let it be.
Land so tender, just like sand.
Oh, be my walking stick.
With Your help, I will not fall
On our solid walk of brick.

As we soon move ahead to know Jesus, let's be reminded that through the cross we find salvation.

Knowing God

On a three-by-seven array so sketched,
"Knowing God" is deeply etched

In a cross that stands out from the board,
Symbolic of our peacemaker Lord.

The two words share the letter *O*.
In opposite direction is their flow.

KnOwing etched down,
GOd spelled left to right.
The cross so prominent is a beautiful sight.

One letter most prominent is the *O*;
Calls me to think of God's love flow.

Circular and perfectly round,
No ending point can be found.

A love that knows not any bound,
And through the cross our salvation is found.

```
        K
        N
 G  G O W  D
        I
        N
        G
```

John 3:16 says, "For God so loved the world that he gave his one and only Son, that whoever believes in him shall not perish but have eternal life."

Let's move on to "Be Still and Know Jesus."

Remember Jesus as the Prince of Peace.

Isaiah 9:6 says, "For to us a child is born, to us a son is given, and the government will be on his shoulders. And he will be called Wonderful Counselor, Mighty God, Everlasting Father, Prince of Peace."

Remember Him

Jesus, as the chosen One,
Heavenly Father's Son.

"Born to be a king,"
Everyone does sing.

Jesus, just Your very name,
Savior, One who came
To deliver and to save
So our faith will not cave.

For we will surely falter
And be confused by the unseen
As we assemble life's puzzle pieces
And learn what they all mean.

When the picture does not feel complete,
Return to kneel at Jesus's feet.

Consider Him that missing piece.
Remember Him, the Prince of Peace.

Remember the almighty cross.

Hebrews 12:2 says, "Fixing our eyes on Jesus, the pioneer and perfecter of faith. For the joy set before him he endured the cross, scorning its shame, and sat down at the right hand of the throne of God."

On the Wood

As we look at our own hands and feet,
And at how we feel when we suffer pain,
Remember Jesus was a real human,
Whose blood shed by vessel and vein.

His hands and feet bore pain
From nails driven deep into His skin,
Pierced into a splintered cross.
We're reminded to cast out sin.

He bore such sorrow in His final days
So we may have joy; thus, rejoice always.

To carry on showing benevolent mercy,
Thanks, and gentleness;
The kindness of a humanitarian
With a spirit of tenderness.

In all things you do,
Seek to promote good.
Remember the vision of the cross,
The crucifixion on the wood.

Be still and remember the birth of Jesus.

Matthew 1:23 says, "'The virgin will conceive and give birth to a son, and they will call him Immanuel,' which means 'God with us.'"

Somewhere Christmas Blooms

Lo, how a rose e'er blooming
Somewhere,
Away in a manger;
Love came down at Christmas
By a holy babe, first a stranger.

What child is this?
Somewhere,
Visited by three kings;
Out of the orient,
Hark, a herald angel sings.

The first noel
Somewhere,
In Bethlehem, O little town;
Sing we now of Christmas;
The angel of the Lord came down.

While shepherds watched their flocks
Somewhere,
It was a silent night, holy night;
Rock-a-bye, dear little boy,
In the manger on that night.

Be still and remember the death of Jesus.

John 19:17 says, "Carrying his own cross, he went out to the place of the Skull (which in Aramaic is called Golgotha)."

Somewhere Golgotha

Somewhere, not just anywhere,
A miracle will happen on a day,
When God interrupts and makes history
With a memory He shall lay,
Revealing God in action,
When all seems rather a hush;
The new miracle will enlighten us,
Like the rising flames of a burning brush.

There's a miracle of holy fire
Celebrated on the same spot and the same day
Throughout many centuries
In the same manner, the same way.

Fire shining down on a little hill,
Believed where Jesus died;
Holy Son, yes, He arose
Three days after He was crucified.

The Holy Land is not just somewhere
But a very special place,
Where fire ignites annually
To remind us of God's grace.

Be still as the Trinity speaks in three persons.

First John 5:6–8 says, "This is the one who came by water and blood—Jesus Christ. He did not come by water only, but by water and blood. And it is the Spirit who testifies, because the Spirit is the truth. For there are three that testify: the Spirit, the water and the blood; and the three are in agreement."

Beyond the Blindfold

Open my eyes that I may see
Beyond the blindfold veiling me.
When it's difficult to visualize life's frame,
Instill me with trust in His holy name.

Open my ears that I may hear
Words that cast out doubt and fear
When I am anxious and so uptight
And do not sleep soundly through the night.

Beyond blinded eyes and muffled ears
Are open hearts and hands,
Ever so gentle and tender,
Offering support like unbroken strands.

For the strand of you and me
Is strengthened evermore
By Jesus's very presence
That keeps the strand so pure.

Reminds us there's a you and me
And the Spirit of a third affinity:
Father, Son, Holy Ghost.
Bond the strand in loving Trinity.

Be still and know Jesus will carry you when walking feels like a trial.

Matthew 11:28 says, "Come to me, all you who are weary and burdened, and I will give you rest."

A Walk in the Sand

Feeling warped and bent out of shape?
Seeking quiet time and a personal escape?

When no one seems to say the right thing,
When you're distracted by your own shortcoming.

Thing, thing. What are the right things?
The magic gift you hope someone brings.

Are they psalms?
Extended palms?
Hugs from warm hands?
Walks in the sands?

Remember the footsteps in sands so white,
When you saw just one set from your very own sight.

When you were carried in times of trial
Upon Jesus's shoulders for mile and mile.

This most blessed escape
Rests your soul and reshapes,
Renews your spirit
To walk next time stronger,
After quiet time with Jesus,
Your strides have grown longer.

Be still and know Jesus is the "light of the world."

John 8:12 says, "When Jesus spoke again to the people, he said, 'I am the light of the world. Whoever follows me will never walk in darkness, but will have the light of life.'"

Rain and Reign

Peaceful rain, oh peace reign.
Serenely shower, serenity power.
Over all, reigning tall.
Clouds burst, rains fall.
Clouds fade to shining sun;
Prince of Peace, oh Holy Son;
Illuminating holy light
That rains and reigns, rays so bright.

Be still and know that Jesus knocks.

Revelation 3:20 says, "Here I am! I stand at the door and knock. If anyone hears my voice and opens the door, I will come in and eat with that person, and they with me."

One Who Knocks

When I'm set back,
Do not attack.
It's just a phase,
My reverted ways.
Can't fast-forward
Like a TV remote.
Must run the course,
Spend time to devote.
Even visit the past
For a very good reason.
Learn something new
From an elusive season,
As if mysteries once were
And still exist;
That could be answered
And cast a new twist—
To my life and even yours,
While God is opening the right doors.
Without latches, knobs, and locks,
Let Jesus in, the "One who knocks."

Seek to follow Jesus. He is our solitary need between God and man.

John 14:6 says, "Jesus answered, 'I am the way and the truth and the life. No one comes to the Father except through me.'"

With One Need

Barring all the pains.
Erasing discolored stains.
When colors run and bleed,
Blur my wants and need.

Wants that seem so many.
Needs reduced to one.
In a defining moment,
Seeking Father's Son.

To help me see through new eyes
What means the most and glorifies.

To help me hear through new ears
Comforting words that quell all fears.

To help me speak with a new voice
Languages that project my choice.

For the One I follow,
A need to gratify.
Living day by day,
To richly satisfy.

Call out to God and Jesus when needed. They clear clouds to help you find your way when you feel lost.

My Defenses

God, Your child is calling You
As tears roll down my face.
Won't You please reach out to me
A hand I can embrace?

The pit from which I find myself
Digging without clear senses;
Naked do I often feel,
Armed without defenses.

Give me a voice that I might say
The right words I truly do hear;
When I'm lost and not quite found,
I'll listen far or near.

Give me eyes that I might see
The right vision, not a delusion;
Clear the clouds that block the way.
See reality, not just an illusion.

Give me a touch, a feeling inside.
Discernment do I need
To better know the right from wrong;
Mistakes held back don't bleed.

How can I serve You better
When it seems I struggle within?
Hard to not be self-centered,
Flesh encased from outside in.

But Jesus, Your Son, paved a path
For mankind since His day.
The body made whole and protected;
Sins do wash away.

So give me the faith to seek You out,
Gain power, strength, and trust.
Escape a pit with pitfalls as I rise
So the stones will scatter like dust.

Be still and know God as Jesus saw God, His almighty Father.

Remember Jesus's words to His disciples.

Matthew 19:26 says, "Jesus looked at them and said, 'With man this is impossible, but with God all things are possible.'"

Seek God and Jesus, for they are perfect love.

King of Kings

He who is perfect goodness,
From whom we are all so imaged,
Yet one we've never seen,
And we long to see His visage.

He's the perfect love at first sight,
Who validates our very thoughts.
If He appeared this very day,
We'd easily feel unkempt in knots.

For we know we're really messy
On the inside and outside,
Seeking to be dressier
With moral traits we do not hide.

As if life is a journey
To reclothe and redress,
Transform messy into dressy,
A royal blessedness.

To stand a royal and regal stance
That can't be paralleled,
Not even by our kings and queens
Before us who have dwelled.

Except for His Son, Jesus,
Who is also a King of Kings;
Praise we repeat with devotion,
Resound in songs we sing.

"King of Kings," we echo.
"Lord of Lords," we sing.
Clothe and dress me in righteousness
That outshines any diamond ring.

Even the rings between bride and groom
Are expressing their souls' undying love;
But the only perfect eternal love
Is given from Him above.

From day of birth to day of death,
He knows each and every one.
From crown of head to tips of toes,
His image breathed in daughter and son.

For this very reason,
God perfects perfect love;
For His love for you preceded
His creation of you from above.

For you and I were once but dust,
And to dust we shall return;
Like Adam and Eve who wore fig leaves,
They reclothed to repent in turn.

Aware of wrongdoing,
They realized they were naked;
So they sought to cover a mistake
For the apple they had tasted.

Don't we all seek a royal dress
To cloak the knots of sin?
But realize God untangles those knots,
And that's where we begin.

Before we move on to knowing yourself, I share the revision of one of my very first poems. I originally titled it To Know Thyself and I treasure that version and will share its original lines as well.

To Know You, God

I don't know where I'm going,
But I know I'm on my way.
I'll take with me my hopes and dreams
Of tomorrow and today.

My memories, both good and bad,
Will always be with me
As I walk along a windy road
To be happy, wise, and free.

And when obstacles get in my way
And sometimes get me down,
I'll try to change my attitude,
Put on a smile, and wipe away my frown.

For accepting what I cannot change
And changing what I can
Within this vast imperfect world
Must go hand and hand.

Of all the things that I've been taught, experienced, seen, and heard,
To know You, God, and that You know best
Is the greatest lesson I have learned.

I originally wrote the last set of lines as you see below. At the time, I chose the word *thyself* as a combined form of *myself* and *thy*. I thought about God as *Thine*; therefore, *Thyself* was my way to refer to the inner living spirit.

Of all the things that I've been taught, experienced, seen, and heard,
To know Thyself and what is best
Is the greatest lesson I have learned.

I realized there were times when I didn't know the best action to take and whether my choices would be fruitful and rewarding. I changed the poetic words to emphasize reliance on God who always knows what is best for me.

Let's proceed to "Be Still and Know Yourself."

You are your own individual in every sense of the word. Be reminded that God knows you better than you know yourself. He knows your thoughts, even before you speak them.

Be authentically true as you find and make your ways through the unique circumstances that define your life. Thank God no matter what these circumstances are and appreciate your wonderful gift of life.

As you journey for self-discovery and inner peace, allow yourself precious moments of stillness.

Much happens during stillness beyond what we are even aware of. God is fully aware. Have you noticed that you may not react until a great jolt causes you to act? Have you wondered about all those happenings you missed during still times?

When the River Is Low

Did you ever watch the river rise
As rain fell down from blackened skies?
Then suddenly the lightning bolt
Struck an object with a great jolt.
Was it the great oak by the shore?
Someone's home struck at the front door?
The jolt woke us up, and so we did run
To witness firsthand what damage was done.
Did you ever wonder why it takes a jolt
To make you move and act with a bolt?
So much happens when the river is low.
The river calls out, "Be still and know."

Appreciate those times when you were favored and something unexpected and special happened to you.

Because

Why did I get chosen?
Random as it was.
I guess I'll have to accept
It simply is "because."
When *because* is our only answer
To "Why me?" "Why now?" just "Why?"
There's randomness in circumstance;
Events may go awry.

135

Sometimes to reap more, you must let nagging preconceptions go.

One of the Crowd

Have you preconceived an in crowd
And set yourself apart?
Distinguishing on some basis
That's matterless from the start.
Imagine you're just one of the crowd,
Alike and all the same,
Seeking affiliation
And friends who are glad you came.

Let your inner light shine and smile.

The Unconditional Smiles

Let go of expectations.
Disappointments can really hurt,
As if you're hungry and thirsty
Or naked with no shirt.
Life may bring us to our knees,
Crawling on our hands,
Feeling like helpless children,
Sinking in murky sands.
Sometimes we get muddy
And carry our grime and dirt,
Reluctant to believe in goodness
And cleanse sins from our shirts,
As if the shirts that we outwardly wear
Are judged by others in such awkward stare,
When what's inside is what counts.
To let your light shine before fear mounts.
Your own self-fear can push you way down
And suddenly turn your smile to a frown.
On a day when you catch yourself sad,
Remember yesterdays' smiles worn so glad,
When the smiles were effortless
And not like a test,
When the smiles were natural,
Unconditional, their best.

You learn important lessons along the way. Look at the big picture of life.
Life is memories. Do see the forest for the trees.

Life

Sometimes things in life must give
To move beyond stagnation.
Sometimes you need a motivating drive
To surpass imagination.

Don't be scared of a challenge.
Don't ever shrink in fear.
Do your best; sincerely try.
Hold what you learn dear.

Lessons learned are important.
Share them when you can.
Promote success of others
As part of your regular plan.

Imparting wisdom to others
Is a blessing and is kind.
Teaching is rewarding,
Enriching to the mind.

Think about life in a simple way,
Making memories every day.

Life: remember lessons when you failed.
Life: remember not to get derailed.

Life: it goes on day by day.
Life: take a moment just to say,

Life is:

Lessons learned,
Ideas shared,
Failures experienced,
Experiences remembered.

Remember those special lessons parents taught you.

Plain Little Lessons

The things we remember our parents so taught,
The things we should do and the things we should not.

Remember your manners with "Thank you" and "Please."
Count your blessings and pray on your knees.

Wipe your feet and make your bed.
Don't worry and fret; go to sleep, sleepyhead.
Don't talk with your mouth full.
Get ready for school.
Hang up your clothes.
Blow your runny nose.

Clean dirty dishes and put them away.
Sing birthday wishes on one's special day.
Say hello and say good-bye.
The list we remember—oh my, oh my.

These life's little lessons, so common but true,
Plain like the colors of red, white, and blue.

Never stop learning. Never stop sharing.

Perpetually Learn and Share

If I could be a perpetual student,
Growing ever so wise and ever so prudent,
Learning so much there is to know,
Seeking more wherever I go.
Traveling here, traveling there,
Always astute, sharp, and aware.
Ready to help you think and grow
As I navigate and learn,
I must apply knowledge I have gained
And give back when it's my turn.
I need to put my knowledge to use;
To waste it away is just no excuse.
Life is more than making the grade.
Let's learn and share in a perpetual fair trade.

Learn from mistakes to be better prepared the next time. Think of "Ready, set, go" as a regimen of personal fitness.

Set to Go

Let me teach the knowledge I've learned
From those mistakes I've overturned.

I'll teach about courage,
Teach about will,
Ask you to relax,
And just be still.

To not rush,
To not hurry,
To not gyrate
On what was blurry.

What did you fail to see before
That blurred your vision and action?
Were you so set on victory
That only winning meant satisfaction?

Well, to set the record straight,
You sometimes fail and have to wait.

You learn so much when you fail
To be ready next time and set to sail.

"Get ready. Get set. Go!"
When you hear the whistle blow,
Telling you a chance so lies
Right before your very eyes.

139

Some of our most precious learning time is spent in quiet moments ... simple time all alone.

Yours Alone

Divert attention from distracting noise
That tempts you like alluring decoys.

Noise is like a decoy to entice.
A decoy confuses and makes you think twice.

Quietness is learning if you will let it be,
When you're guided by faith and not by what you see.

It's perfectly okay to live with some blinders
And not get off course by noisy side winders.

Let the quiet be soothing away from alarm,
Quiet and protective, feeling safe from all harm.

It's simple time you cannot clone
When the moments are yours and yours alone.

During special moments, seek to know your authentic self. This is who you are in your core.

Seek and Find

Know your authentic "self,"
So very real and true,
For God, the Most High,
Is looking out for you.
He won't reject. He won't displace.
He'll hold you with loving grace.
When you hide behind a mask,
God desires you take the next task,
So outlined as to seek and find,
A small brave step to clear your mind;
To seek and find who you're created to be,
Then to live that "self" so wonderfully.

So dive into your core and peel back the layers.

Deeply Lies a Core

The very word *core*,
The center of matter,
The crux and heart,
The former and latter.
Were you ever asked who you are in your core,
Then find yourself peeling back layers some more?
Finding your core reminds us so
Of studying ourselves from head to toe,
Asking, "Where is it that I am weak?
How do I function at my peak?
Where do I fail yet wish to excel?
Where do I win, succeed so well?"
The inner matter,
The utmost core,
Deeply lies a hidden store
Of secrets and keys to who you are,
Reveals your fire as a shining star.

If you make changes in your life, be true to yourself and be comfortable with change.

Rich Spirits

I shall not ask for more
Than for you to be from your core,
For if you change for me,
You lose your identity.
Being someone you're not
Puts you on the spot.
But if you change for you,
How we seem so true.

Likewise in reverse,
Let me requote the verse.
You shall not ask of me
To be more than I can be,
For when I'm from my core,
My spirit's rich, not poor.
And if I change for me,
How blessed we both will be.

Remember, you aren't perfect. Embrace imperfection.

Embrace Imperfection

Strive for a perfect heart.
Settle for imperfect actions.
Be kind and good to others.
Be alert to unavoidable distractions.

Stay focused on your goals.
Strive to do your best.
Use your time wisely.
It's yours to fully invest.

Don't forget yourself.
You deserve self-kindness too.
Be compassionate and patient.
Don't bite off more than you can chew.

Strive for perfect actions.
Desire a perfect heart.
Accept kindness of others
That they offer and impart.

Embrace imperfection.
Recognize wrongdoings and flaws.
Flaws come in many flavors,
And that's just natural law.

Be your own best friend. Make peace with yourself.

Candle Glow, Hourglass Flow

When all you can think about is survival,
But all you can be is your own worst rival.

When the candle seems to burn at both ends,
But you haven't learned to be your best friend.

When life spirals down like the sands in an hourglass,
Turn the glass over, dream on, let the hours pass.

The nightmares so troubling are a thing of the past.
Worries about the future are not even so vast.

With the glass turned over,
Inverted sands flow to the downside,
Though a journey on a roller coaster
Is a sinuous chase on a thrill ride.

A roller coaster life, hectic and frenzied,
Ever so wild and fast;
The hourglass is patient and slow,
Ever in control in contrast.

The perfect time it so keeps,
Each grain in peaceful accord;
Much different than your old track
Of intensity and discord.

Don't let time run out.
Keep the sand ever flowing.
....
......
....
..
The candle doesn't have to burn out.
Relight an end, see it glowing.

Peace is keeping an open mind for future chances. Open doors are worth the wait.

Time Awaiting

Ticktock, ticktock.
I wish I could turn back the clock
To a time when I was about to err,
Running rampant, do as I dare;
Not considering the long-term impacts,
Confused by bewildering information and facts.

No time is nil nor insignificant.
All time does matter,
Even when we have misapprehensions
And a bit of reckless mind chatter.

For when the mind talks and thinks of regret,
It fears future chances not realized yet.
Those future chances are your open doors,
Where all that you wanted awaits to be yours.

Realize you change and grow. A time will come when you are ready to break new ground and new clay.

The One

High upon a mountaintop,
I then begin to fall.
Stranded in the valley,
My name it is I call.

I hear the echoes
Ringing in my ears.
I listen for the right one
To wipe away my tears.

I'm not the one from the past,
Nor the one I am today.
I seek her out—she is real,
The one who breaks the clay.

A time will come when you want to move from sinking sand to solid ground and get beyond those things holding you back that you dwell on.

Glory Bound

One day I wasn't feeling well.
Seems I could only dwell and dwell.
After a while, I felt so low.
I quickly jumped and shouted, "Whoa!"
Sometimes it takes a stopping hand
To not drift into sinking sand,
To plant your feet on solid ground,
To not feel lost but glory bound.

A time will come when you are ready to lighten your load and turn your burdens over to God.

A Less-Crooked Road

Heavy burdens are too much weight.
Learn to lighten the load.
Lay your burdens at God's feet.
Travel a less-crooked road.

For burdens are like forks,
When you must make a choice
To clear out the excess baggage,
To attune more to God's voice.

Following a much straighter path,
As your forks look more like knives;
With clarity and linear direction,
You follow how God drives.

A time will come when you feel assured that your time is coming.

Deferred and Assured

I'm not defeated. I'm deferred.
My time's coming. I'm assured.

I'm protected behind a shield
Till it's time to reap God's yield.

A time when stress has turned to ease,
And I stand openly as I please;
Beyond the comfort zone, I've found
Grace and joy that are not bound.

God's supply does not run out
When increased demand for Him we shout.

With growing comes stumbling. Imagine looking back at your life and times of wobbliness.

Through Trials

Be still at dawn.
Be still and know.
Just watch the fawn
Grow into a doe.

As she matures
With effortless grace,
Any wobbly step
Is her own pace.

She may fall and frequently stumble,
But her pride won't let her crumble.

When she matures,
She'll find a buck,
Who gracefully grew
Through trials, not luck.

Realize you wear your inner ego and spirit on the outside. Let your heart be full regardless of any dress with which you are clothed.

Heart of the Fullness

Jagged, torn britches
In need of stitches;
Multicolored threads
To mend fabric shreds.

Ripped-apart seams
That don't destroy dreams;
Outerwear that appears tattered.
An inner self in no way shattered.

An inner ego strong and intact
As the dress is all just a shield,
Covering up what lies within;
The heart of the fullness, the yield.

Let your spirit and conscience speak to you like an inner voice of wisdom deep within.

Inner Spirit, Inner Voice

The courageous human spirit
That outlives a tragedy
Is a voice of wisdom
And attests to reality.

A role model of strength and triumph,
Perhaps one we'd call a saint;
Or maybe a guardian angel
Blessed with wings if we could paint.

Wings to remind us
That we can fly and soar
Above our private battles
And exit stronger than before,
Relying on our spirit
That dwells so deep inside;
That inner voice we listen to
And at the same time so confide.

147

Realize your own self-worth and value as you develop mutual love with others.

Mutuality

Oh, let me make a difference
Beyond the Ping-Pong ball
going
... back
and
forth ...

From table side to table side,
For I possess and realize
Value called "self-worth,"
Value in my eyes,
God-given worth to me;
Not a Ping-Pong ball controlled
By players;
One on one,
You see.
I am not that ball controlled
By the mercy of the situation on the table;
Being bounced
... to one side
then the other ...
Until a player is not stable.
A player will drop the ball,
Then lose that very round,
But my self-worth propels me,
For with God I'm never lost but found.
The Ping-Pong ball so teaches us about
Flowing love and connection.
For a Ping-Pong ball always
d
r
o
p
s

And loses to-and-fro direction.
So work on developing mutual love,
Not like the flow across a net;
But between two loving people
Who grow to bond since they have met.

When days feel so hectic and busy, find the time of day to catch your breath and help another do the same. Ride the waves of life together.

A Time of Day

Let me find a time of day
Just to catch my breath.
Once I've finally caught it,
Let me feel its breadth.

Rhythmically, it sings a song,
Narrow or wide, short or long.

Let me find a time of day
To help another do the same,
Another who is needy,
Who's thankful that I came.

For a storm will pass,
As we ride its wave.
Hand in hand together,
We will be so brave.

As long as we hold hands so tight,
No storm will overcome our might.

As you deepen your spiritual maturity, flow with God like a circle. Journey boundlessly.

The Shape I Am In

Today I look at myself, agape,
As if I can define a geometrical shape,
Like a triangle with lines that don't meet;
Disconnecting intersections, I fall to my feet.

If I were a shape that sits on a scale,
The scale may tip heavy with my extra pail.

That pail I've held with my burdens enclosed,
When to lose the weight, I should really disclose;
Inner thoughts and feelings stored away
In that pail that made me pale today.

For God can help me empty the pail,
Reshape me for the next time I sit on the scale.

On a day, the balance I seek will feel right,
Points all connected, aligned in my sight.
Will I become a triangle that day?
Life is flowing, a circle I'll play.

So as I journey without a life map,
It's nice to get caught in a circular wrap.
No roads stopping at corner points.
One flowing line is devoid of three joints.

"Not at all ironic," I say.
Look to "The Way."
Look to that day!

Seek out
your circle.
Be it always!

Envision your journey taking you up a ladder, much like a stairway reaching toward heaven.

I Want to Climb

Out of my sight, you are,
But I know you're near, not far.
I want to climb into your arms.
Be not afraid of any harms.

Sometimes in my older age,
I revert to memories of a much younger stage;
With the innocence I felt when I was young,
Learning to climb steps, each ladder's next rung.

Ladders are generally used to climb up,
But they can help reach the depths of pits,
The valleys we find ourselves mentally in
When low and losing our wits.

Life so differs from an extension ladder
That we extend and then pull back,
A physical ladder we climb lower or higher
By a definite leaning track.

The ladder I write and speak of here
Is about growth, how you like to define;
Perhaps that passing with age
Or a spiritual path much like an incline.

To take you higher, higher,
Embarking to serve God,
Wholeheartedly and willingly taking new steps
Upon heaven's stairway that we applaud.

Sometimes climbing a ladder is just like taking unchartered, scary steps. You are just an average, ordinary person. Everyone feels fears.

The Ladder in the Street

Just a man in the street.
Ordinary and quite the average?
A man is but the product of his thoughts.
What he thinks, he becomes, like the adage.

What does he dream when he's alone?
What's his vision all his own?
Not that of which the world perceives
But what he thinks as he so sees.

> When he's feeling low,
> He may be swept off his feet,
> Just sitting at the bottom rung
> Of a ladder in the street.

He hangs out by the bottom rung
With a golden, silent tongue.
Maybe he can't define his dreams,
Or "out to dry" he now feels hung.

> When he's feeling high,
> He may be swept off his feet,
> Clinging to the highest rung
> Of a ladder in the street.

He hangs out by the uppermost rung
With the upper hand,
Feeling in charge of his dreams
Like a leader in command.

> This ordinary man
> Could be surely insecure.
> This very same man
> Could be just average; He's obscure.

> I would say that any man
> Has his personal lows and highs.
> Somewhere on the ladder in the street
> Fear of the unknown takes him by surprise.

When you try something new, a feeling of nervousness is very real. How common it is to say, "I've got butterflies in my stomach."

Butterfly Feelings

When every new adventure
Feels like your first plane flight,
Waiting to break through the clouds
And catch your line of sight.
Every new adventure is a new dawn on the rise.
Will you face it head on or cower with ifs and whys?
New jobs, new friends,
New homes, new trends.
What's around upcoming bends?
What's in store?
More than before?
Grace and gratitude galore?
As your adventure settles
Like the landing of the flight,
The butterflies you felt inside
Fly quickly out of sight.
Butterfly feelings that flitter and jitter
Make you dizzy like dancing stars glitter.

As you embark to serve God, think about how you can be a disciple and serve others. Promote your fruits of labor.

Get Going

Commend thy efforts and all successes.
But why stop there?
Command more efforts and new successes.
By why go there?
The road doesn't stop at a red light,
Neither at yellow nor green.
There lies a fruitful path ahead
For benefits yet unseen.
Promote the fruits of labor
And do not waste your gifts.
Your talent, skills, and aptitude
Are your "get going" shifts.

As you serve God, carry an attitude of God-centeredness. Ask yourself, "How can I serve God today?"

If I?

Have you ever noticed that words that end with i-f-y
Can easily be self-directed, so you may ask "If I?"

If I could only
Rectify errors,
Pacify terrors,
Modify behavior,
Glorify our Savior,
Testify to God's glory,
Simplify life's story.

Sanctify sinners,
Make them feel like winners,
Dignify those oppressed,
Make them feel less depressed,
Gratify one's desires and what he or she admires,
Purify the unclean so they're proud to be seen,
Beautify from the inside out,
Nullify your every doubt.

Magnify our Lord,
Fortify others' faith.
If I could replace self-centeredness with God-centeredness,
Then I've served well, I saith.

Walk gracefully in a beauty walk, remembering God as your greatest beholder. Walk in accordance to His commandments.

Beauty is in the eye of the beholder.

Our Beauty Walk

Beauty pleases our senses.
True beauty runs deeper than skin.
The beauty God, our maker, eyes
Is the gentle, quiet spirit from within.

A spirit like fine virtue,
More appealing than allure.
We are not all pageant beauty queens,
Yet beauty consumes us for sure.

Our supreme spectator, who sits upon the throne,
Beholds and eyes each heart, which each calls "my own."

He holds the supreme vantage point.
He observes and misses no mark,
Watching the intentions of all hearts,
Never losing sight in light or dark.

We as human people, yes, we miss the mark.
We sin by human nature and stumble in the dark.

Sometimes we veer from the beauty path
Of principles we are commanded to live by;
In those times, we need to turn stained beauty
Into that more acceptable to God's eye.

Look at each day as a beauty walk,
Stepping gracefully to avoid mess,
Taking steps to allow a pure heart
To shine like prayers we so confess.

Let's move forward to "Be Still and Know Others."

Have you thought about the concept of friends of the road and friends of the heart? A friend of the road may walk with you for a while, but then your journey together loses connection. A friend of the heart touches you in a deeper way. Such a friend touches your heart so deeply, allowing you to connect with an unbreakable bond and genuine depth.

Recognize friendship is a gift beyond compare.

Open It Up

Is friendship not a science but an art
Where emotions connect deep in the heart?

Friendship is like an arena to play.
Let your guard down and know it's okay.

Withstanding drama, sharing the laughter.
Whatever emotion before, now, and after.

Friendship stands the test of time
Deep within the soul,
Overcoming periods of complexity
When it feels you've hit a black hole.

Instead let that hole reveal
Something about yourself.
When friendship deserves more than a chance
Than tucked upon a shelf.

Open it up like a dusty book
That seldom you may read.
And all in all, the characters revive
And find that they do need;
To mend a hole in the heart
That started with a drift.
To finally say, "I miss you."
You've recognized friendship's gift.

We form first impressions but look beyond initial thoughts to deeply get to know others.

Beneath Topsoil and Skin

Would you walk away from a garden of weeds
Or pluck one by one to see what it needs?

Would you discover what's beneath topsoil,
Despite long hours of labor and toil?

Would you rake, dig, and plow the earth?
Bonding to land and all that it's worth;

And if that land were people instead,
Would you look beyond first impression?
Maybe you walked away too soon
Without seeking for deeper dimension.

You may find beauty in the depths of the earth,
And sure, you'll find bugs and worms too.
But human beauty lies deeper than the skin—
The top transparency for goodness to shine through.

We all have a story and saga to share.

The Eyes Story

Did my eyes reveal a story
Or simply a blank stare?
Did you look through windows
To see sagas that they bare?

Did I see in your eyes
A story of your own?
Did my eyes get past your hue
To sagas you have known?

As if our eyes could bind us
Like strangers newly met,
Unveiling innermost emotions
As a windows-to-souls duet.

Sow seeds of kindness. Kindness is a direct route to one's heart.

Jump Start to My Ears

Supplant my worn-out routines
Like I replace torn shoes.
Deliver to my mail drop
Wonderful seeds of good news.

My mail drop doesn't have to be
The physical box that you do see,
Standing at the driveway's end
Just around the highway's bend.

No, there is a more direct route
Conveying your message out.
Just drop kind words into my heart,
The mailbox that sparks my jump and start.

When I hear that wonderful voice I know,
I can feel my emotions on the rise and go.
The greatest jump start to my ears
That brings a smile and wipes away tears.

Sometimes you give more. Sometimes you receive more.

Happy States, Happy Faces

If you constantly seek approval,
Others may return rejection,
Giving you the opposite
In a hopeless state of dejection.
Rejection, never, not, and no.
Careless words when careful goes.
Out of our conscience for a while,
Until we regroup a more caring style.
A style for two to be positive;
The one who receives
And the one who will give.
For the next time around,
The two may switch places,
Exchanging positives,
Happy states, happy faces.

Let kindness help put out fires and soften hearts when there is communication breakdown. As I wrote this poem, I thought about the importance of drinking water, and I jotted down the following prescription:

Water thy tongue for when water flows in the mouth, no unkind words can flow out. And if they do, you can't understand them because they are so watered down and not fired up!

SOS Please

Have I added more fuel to a wee small flame
That set a fire ablaze?
Have I added more fuel to a big burning fire
That set our minds in craze?

A small flame can be contained
From a mouth with a tiny blow.
But an out-of-control fire
Will take much more to quiet and mellow.

Sowing with nurturing words and seeds
To bloom speech spoken with kindness;
To soothe and soften communication
And reach a point of like-mindedness.

Soothe and soften heard another way
May sound like an SOS call—
Save Our Souls, a cry for help,
Before fire makes us fall.

Communication breakdown
That drops us to our knees;
Like a point in time for prayer
To be heard with the word "please."

So when there's fire in a room,
Or voices clash and so do loom,
Stop, drop, and from your knees,
In a humbled position,
Say, "SOS please."

Words sometimes get misunderstood and misinterpreted. Clear the air to dispel tension and work toward the common good.

Common Good

Misperception and misinterpretation.
True and false at the same time.
One views things one way;
The other may in time.
When two finally catch up
And clear the sultry air,
Realizing unguarded thoughts of both
Were not watched by their eyes' stare.
Watch your thoughts; think before you speak
Before accusing words start to leak.
The underlying truth of communication: "Things will get misunderstood."
But to clear up any falsehoods is for everyone's common good.

Friendship barriers may feel like solid doors when we really are seeking friends to support us like solid floors.

As Solidness Melts

Be still when you are not quite sure
If you must close a solid door.
For once you close and walk away,
You may pine for yesterday.

For over time that solid door
May support you like a solid floor,
Like an old friend
You didn't see clearly,
But stayed in your heart
To love now so dearly.

Solidness may melt
Like barriers torn apart
When solid becomes clear
As the window of your heart.

So open the window
And don't shut the door.
Let fresh air and hope
Circulate and restore.

Once hurtful words are spoken, a relationship needs healing time. Relationships worth holding onto work out over time, and hearts grow dear and near.

Dear and Near

Say what you mean.
Mean what you say.
Don't let another's words
Lead you astray.

Words can hurt deeper than guns and knives,
Wreaking havoc in each other's lives,
Especially when there is love and care.
An inappropriate word is a lie that you share.

It hurts to be spoken.
It hurts to be heard.
Don't let mutual trust
Fly away like a bird.

But if it so happens and love seems to have flown,
Give it some time to heal and atone.

Don't shrink and feel small.
Don't tower or feel tall.

Believe you may see
Eye to eye and agree.
The relationship is dear.
Your hearts will grow near.

Treasure bonds you have formed with friends and honor commitments.

For if We Hear

Perhaps I saw so many fumbles.
Oh, how my heart crumbles.
Did second-guessing become innate
When my choices weren't so great?
But that is all a question, you see,
Relevant to circumstances that be,
For time can change and rearrange
A waiting pattern that feels so strange.
While things are being worked on and worked out,
Commitment, my friend, is what it's about.
For if I hear you and you hear me,
It does not matter what our eyes see.
For then we trust a positive outcome
Worth all the pain and strain,
For then we believe a bond has formed
And carried us through the rain.

Remember the importance and value of teamwork.

An Apple Cart Shared

Have I spoiled a workable plan? Upset the apple cart?
Devised my own initiative to fire like a dart?
Remember back to a simple time
When the goal was to shine at all costs.
It didn't matter how you played the game
When victory could not be tossed.
As you were determined to win for you
And forgot about your team;
Recognition was your prize,
Or so you thought it seemed.
You didn't want to share.
Teamwork was not your pride.
You sought the commendation
With no one by your side.
It took some time to understand.
Togetherness wins over triumphs gained on your own.
An apple cart shared is no team member spared.
Others matter and don't leave each other alone.

163

When additional storms arise, face those storms together.

Face a Storm

When noise gets in the way,
It's harder to hear what you're trying to say.
That's when benefit of doubt should reign
So every word doesn't sound like "complain."
When you accept another and unconditionally care,
You'll truly see that relationship is rare,
For commitment may not be our typical norm.
We often walk away and don't face a storm.

Remember the importance of sensitivity and consider others' feelings.

Walk on a Balance Beam

Take a walk on a balance beam.
Not so easy as it seems.
Take care in every step in sight,
Lest you fall to left or right.

Life is such a balancing act,
Considering others and using tact.
Gauging others' sensitive spots,
What they'll brush off and what they will not.

For communicating is just a walk,
Learning to respect our mutual talk.

For when others are mad at you,
A hurdle takes the beam's place,
Leaving you so ever tongue tied,
Taking care in every pace.

Caution to avoid a crashing fall
Or coming up just short.
Watching what you say next time
To avoid a verbal retort.

So as you eye the hurdle,
Remember to be sensitive to others' feelings.
But if you fall down, get up again.
Set your sights on friendship healings.

Remember the importance of empathy. What if you took a walk in someone else's shoes? You might be surprised by what you come to learn.

A New Language

Oh, you have a way with words,
But are you making a point?
When you are not self-restraining,
Your words do disappoint.
What good is a yell, a slander, a curse?
Better take time to rehearse.
Communicate with self-control,
Eloquence, style, and grace.
Communicate without control
Shows anger to displace.
Think about your counterpart,
To whom you so relate.
A language of peace and empathy—
With that you must translate.
As if you feel for the other,
Step inside his or her shoe.
Take a walk, and you just might
Find out what you never knew.

Keep promises, especially to your married spouse.

Loving Oaths and Vows

When you find a partner,
For whom oaths you share,
If ever a word is broken,
Tell the other then and there.
When you find a partner,
For whom vows you esteem,
If ever a word is misleading,
Don't fill assumptions in between.
The in-between-the-lines spaces
Are where we fill each other's gaps.
The story grows ever wider,
Leading to misperceptions and mishaps.
Promises are important,
Words exchanged so clearly.
Communicate, not alienate,
And love each other dearly.

Be comfortable in shared moments of silence.

When Nothing Is Everything

When I really know you,
I don't need to see; I can hear.
From afar you are,
Yet you are ever near.

When I really know you,
I don't need to hear; I can see.
From so near you are,
Ever quietly with me.

Sharing that comfortable
Moment of silence
When we gaze or look away;
For at that very moment,
Nothing was all we had to say.

Have you ever wanted to make
Everything out of nothing
When nothing was all we shared?
And that moment meant everything
In that moment we so shared.

Treasure moments to be each other's light. Extend forgiveness to keep love steadfast and glowing like the light of a candle's flame.

Candle Flames

Burnt ashes. Candle flames.
Things we've trashed; things we save.
People we blamed; others forgave.
Times we've stepped on
And should've looked over.
Didn't realize the gift of a rare four-leaf clover.
Some special person,
Some unique friend,
Whose love is steadfast and fully does send
Refreshing light when other candles burn out;
Picks up broken pieces to mend inside out.
Scattered ashes cannot displace
A candle flaming in the right place.

Should you face hatred and unkindness, respond by giving love. Let love be a huge attention-getter.

When Two Cheeks Face

As I travel in my footsteps
Importantly in my mind,
Conscious of my thoughts.
Are they clean and kind?

To be kind in spirit,
From the inside out,
Be patient when I falter,
Not exclaiming words of shout.

Not showing retaliation
But turning the other cheek;
When someone isn't being kind
In the words he or she does speak.

There's a big attention-getter
When one responds to hatred with giving love;
And that's called an opportunity,
Sharing doctrine as the "ahem" words from above.

Wouldn't it be special when a moment unsuspecting
Turns two cheeks to face kindly; so ever unexpecting!

We learn from things we've done wrong. Understand mistakes aren't etched in stone.

To Learn the Hard Way

The writing I write feels right for me. I edit as I go.
To make it ever righter, I write the words to flow.

I speak to myself as I write, enhancing words in tone.
I take this as "experience," not mistakes so etched in stone.

For it would be wrong to keep records—accounts of my wrong.
Love keeps no logbook and history as I move along.

As this has been an important lesson to learn
Not coming easily,
Others may say the same thing:
"This is not a snap for me."

We are prone to judge ourselves and others so alike.
But if we step back and ponder this, here's what this looks like.

Pickiness and pettiness, idle fights where we ache in the end,
When what we truly wanted was relationships as friends.

Suffering through the hardships with others
Is learning the hard way.
But love that is everlasting
Is a love that is meant to stay.

Let's turn our attention to "Faith, Hope, and Love."

In all these relationships I have written about, it's important to realize that important gifts are from God. Faith, hope, and love are guiding principles to help us journey from pebbles to stepping-stones and find safer and more solid ground to place our feet.

First Corinthians 13:13 says, "And now these three remain: faith, hope and love. But the greatest of these is love."

Hebrews 11:1 says, "Now faith is confidence in what we hope for and assurance about what we do not see."

Leap and Walk

To take a leap of faith is to stand, not lean,
To walk in trust, despite what you have seen,
To not be marred and scarred by the past,
But that hope and goodwill be firm and steadfast.
Do you lean upon a crutch,
Unhealthy and excessively depend?
Do you not know where to turn
Or not know God as your friend?
He with everlasting arms
Outstretched to welcome and hold.
You'll find no greater comforter.
His love surrounds so bold.

By taking a leap of faith, you feel a sense of freedom to let go of crutches and see what happens.

Grounded and Free

In a moment you feel dumbfounded.
Picture yourself stable and seamlessly grounded.
Your head may wave like a flag in the breeze.
Your heart may flutter like coasting high seas.
'Neath a waving flag stands a pole: tall and erect.
It towers above you. Point your eyes direct.
Onward and upward, in comparison you're not small.
You can be grounded, not lean to the wall.
Feel free to venture beyond what crutches.
With faith you'll leap high, like a bouncing ball touches.

Faith is trust that good things are in store.

Romans 8:28 says, "And we know that in all things God works for the good of those who love him, who have been called according to his purpose."

For the Good

Things work together for the good,
Like following a recipe.
Right ingredients, Right actions
Blend in harmony.

Trust and do good
When you say something is bad.
To not have something
May be better than you had.

To not have someone
May mean it's just God's delay.
Maybe there's learning and maturing
To reap a relationship meant to stay.

To not see something or someone
Doesn't mean disappearance.
Sure, it's such a quandary
Without sight and mere appearance.

But think about a recipe
And the ingredient so-called time.
No recipe turned out in seconds.
The output took more time.

Faith is trusting in our prayer requests and believing during "enough is enough" times.

Especially Then

Open my eyes to see what's real.
Open my heart to genuinely feel.
Life isn't easy.
Yes, it's tough.
Sometimes we proclaim,
"Enough is enough!"
When burdens are weighty and incredibly tragic,
God's help and redemption are visible, not magic.

You will not see Him physically,
But the results appear each day.
Some new miracle transpires
Beyond "abracadabra" a magician would say.

It comes with faith that we trust
In miracles and what we request in prayer.
We hold no wand, nor chant magic words,
But fold our hands and solemnly do share
Words giving thanks and words requesting
God to look out for us,
Especially in those "enough is enough" times
When we choose to get by with trust.

Renew and refuel faith. It can be easy to slip into a pattern of fear. Swing into faith and be a branch that reaches out to the "Vine."

God Fills

Fear on the run is no fun.
It must be tamed and surely reframed.
As you long and pine as a branch to the Vine,
You eye a monkey that will not stay still.
He's on the move fervently by his inner will.
But your faith needs refueling and regularly fed.
Replace those fears that spin in your head.
Stop swinging like the monkey so scattered.
Invest in faith so fears will be shattered.
For God's promises are the finest will
To feed your spirit and ever fulfill.

Be faithful with a humble spirit.

First Peter 5:6 says, "Humble yourselves, therefore, under God's mighty hand, that he may lift you up in due time."

Pause

Is there a bigger picture?
Is there a higher cause?
Out of such deep questions,
Maybe it's time to pause.
Somewhere between rewind and forward,
There lies the action of pause.
It may sound ever so idle.
Perhaps it is because
We are a people on the move
Who scramble, rush, and hurry.
We are a people often self-absorbed,
Self-centered with our worry.
Chasing the win and victory,
Naturally, we like to compete
Within ourselves and with others
To not feel self-defeat.
But when we choose to pause
And relax our selfish pride,
We'll be fulfilled with humbleness
That's gracious, far, and wide.

Pause in stillness now. Are you taking a deep breath? Let your heart and mind be filled with hope.

Romans 15:13 says, "May the God of hope fill you with all joy and peace as you trust in him, so that you may overflow with hope by the power of the Holy Spirit."

Let your heart and spirit feel cleansed and renewed.

Psalm 51:10 says, "Create in me a pure heart, O God, and renew a steadfast spirit within me."

The next few poems are poetic stories focusing on faith, hope, and love. Have an open heart and mind, and realize you can open doors for others, just as they may do so for you.

My Hope Chest

I dig deeply into my hope chest
On a day set aside for rest.

My hope chest is not a cedar box
Of collectibles and treasured stock.
My hope chest is my beating heart,
My prominent spiritual building block.

Between two shoulders and below my head,
My hope chest is always there
To cultivate and sustain me,
To bear life's wear and tear.

For if I looked into a cedar box, I'd find just tangible things.
But feelings, emotions, and hopes are my dear intangible wings,
As if they were appendages to carry me through flight,
To soar if I am happy or touched with chilling fright.

My hope chest is my beating heart,
My spiritual hub and core,
Not a box of cedar or any wood
Yet fuller than any drawer.

The Sojourner Angel

Open hearts, open minds, open doors.
Faraway places, faraway skies, faraway shores.
Few and far between,
Visible but rarely seen.

The stranger comes, the stranger goes.
Where he roams, nobody knows.

To an open door
On some faraway shore.

Greeted with open heart and mind,
Others are so very kind.

But the stranger doesn't stay.
He roams like a nomad far away.

A sojourner he remains.
We may wonder why,
But the stranger finds his way
By a power in the sky.

The Prayer Twist

"Pastor, is it right to pray
For a simpler, normal way?"
He looked at me and replied.
Then with tears, he so cried.
Many ask that question
As if normal exists;
A condition that they've also sought,
But here's the story's twist.
No one lives by normal.
God planned no definitions.
God is supernatural,
Giving life dynamic conditions.
On that note the pastor so kind
Promised there's no normal to find.
He answered, "It is right to pray."
Then he wiped his tears away.

From Lonely to Only

The solitary man
With the solitary plan
Toiled as a lonely one,
His father's lonely son.
He fought a cause he lost.
He fled from that lost cause.
He took a pause in life
Just to put his life on pause.
As he meditated in rewind,
He soon turned 180 degrees.
He fast-forwarded so quickly
And fell upon his knees.
He sobbed and asked the Father God,
"Oh, what would you have me do?"
Praying on his knees to heal,
His emotions black and blue.
He made a new friend,
God's one and only Son.
Inviting Jesus into his life,
He's no longer a lonely one.

One Spirit

A heart of stone and a heart of glass
Collided on the mountain pass.
Glass was the lass. Stone was the lad.
The glass was good. The stone was bad.
But who's to say what's good or bad?
Labeling might drive you mad.
Where you see glass that can easily break,
Glass may be stronger than the worst mistake.
Where you see stone that won't easily scratch,
Stone may be weaker than a burned-out match.
When lad and lass collided,
The two instantly confided.
They went to the core, searching for more.
In the end, both did break
The outer shells that were so fake.
Their minds were open.
Their hearts were true.
Lad and lass bonded,
One spirit from two.

Wily Spiders

Spider, weave your web for me
Of rare and complex intricacy.

You are born just knowing how
To spin geometry;
Patterns of silk and sticky threads.
Oh, what sovereignty.

Head to the web when you are hungry.
What's caught in the sticky array?
While I head to the grocery store
On some hurried day.

I wasn't watching closely enough
When I made it to the door.
Now I find my hair in a web.
I am the stuck one for sure.

Let that be a lesson for me
And you and you alike.
Watch out for those spider webs,
Those elusive traps that strike.

Much like life as wiles find you
In some persuasive way;
Even from dark corners,
Wily spiders wait to prey.

A spider is there to trap,
Not concerned about your mess.
He would sooner deceive
Than offer any form to bless.

Next time you see a spider web and the master of its art, remember that all woven lines might
deflect a heart. A web is but a network of fine threads we perceive as a trap.

SIFT

Mother and her little girl
Stood in the kitchen sunny.
"Momma, may I have a cup of
Chamomile tea with honey?"
"Yes, my dear, and so you know,
I'm about to make a cake.
I sure could use a pair of hands.
Won't you help me bake?"
Mother reached for flour as she
Had her daughter's attention.
Then she shared a little advice
From her heart to dearly mention.
"Many think *sift* is for flour and sediment.
But what will help you, my dear, is this lifelong regimen.
A screening action to diligently SIFT—Seek Inside, Face Truths;
I know, my young listener, this sounds like work of sleuths,
Like examining your recipe,
The mixture and the fold.
What is it you do see?
The values that you hold,
The inner composition
Like the ingredients in the cake,
Your outer disposition,
The statements you do make.
It can be hard work to turn your eyes inside.
Remember the importance of a healthy sense of pride.
The consistency of flour helps to make the cake.
Carrying a good attitude surely takes the cake,
For taking the cake is like excellence,
Like having and giving a good heart;
Similar to sharing a home-baked cake,
Are you willing to shape another's heart?
You may not always like everything you see.
Every cake may not rise. You shall come to see.
When you *sift*, you can sieve and rid and modify
Those negative behaviors that do not satisfy.
Self-satisfaction is to like and love who you are.
Won't you let sifting be an act to take the cake by far?"

If you were the little girl, what would you have said next? I think I would have said, "I will help,
Momma, but can I lick the bowl and beaters?" Don't we love the sweet stuff?

Blessings are sweet stuff so nice to receive and hear. The following traditional Gaelic blessing prompted me to write the closing poem of this section.

An Irish Blessing

May the road rise up to meet you.
May the wind be always at your back.
May the sun shine warm upon your face,
The rain fall soft upon your fields.
And until we meet again,
May God hold you in the palm of His hand.

In God's Hands

God will do what God will do,
Forge what He intends,
Even though the human mind
Not always comprehends.
He will provide, make a way,
Connect the past to present day,
Pave future roads when we feel lost
To pay the debts of yesteryear cost.
He knows our human nature—
To live by sight, not trust.
He wants to turn those words around
So hopes don't turn to dust.
Behind the scenes, He does fight
Like a warrior with great might,
Shepherding any single sheep
That runs with delusion, loses sleep.
For He cares so deeply with nestling hands that save,
Inviting those who doubt to seek when they're not brave.
God will remind us all, "Do not be afraid."
He will not separate from His people He has made.

Be Still

In Your
Happy Place

Be Still the Dawn

In the "Be Still, Everybody Hurts" section, I mentioned how I view "dawn." Dawn is realization. Reality changes. Each day is new. Each day is a new dawn.

In the "Be Still and Know" section, I invited you to journey with me and start to see things differently.

Now is the time to live for "dawn" and purpose. Time on earth goes quickly. Recall God's first words to Adam and Eve were to "Be fruitful and multiply."
Hold that thought in your mind as you read and reflect in faithfulness.

We know God is present in each surrounding.
The natural and man-made are all so astounding.
He's everywhere all the time. He's that wonderful! He gave us the gift of life.

Matthew 7:7 says, "Ask and it will be given to you; seek and you will find; knock and the door will be opened to you."

Did you notice the three action verbs? Ask, seek, and knock.

We know that everybody hurts. Wouldn't it be wonderful to ask for help during troubled times and to do so very specifically? The verse above states, "It will be given to you."

We need to be still and know. We are commanded to seek. Following seek, our expectation is to find. As we read in the next two Bible verses, we should seek with a passion in our hearts. We should seek God's face. Though we won't see His face, we should seek His presence in our lives. He will give us rest.

Jeremiah 29:13 says, "You will seek me and find me when you seek me with all your heart."

Psalm 105:4 says, "Look to the Lord and his strength; seek his face always."

We have been reminded to knock. This is much different from any tangible door, for which we rap a cupped hand. Now we are knocking as a feeling much like inspiration and calling, as if we've heard God speaking to us and we feel free to reach out. With this freedom, we desire to realize dawn. In fact, we are ready for dawn. We acquire and practice faith, and hope in our future days to come.

In this section, journey with me as we let ourselves feel such important guiding principles for our lives. Allow them to fill your inner being as you act. We've allowed ourselves to feel and be reminded of past pains. We've paused in stillness and heard God's whispering voice. Now that whisper calls. Each day is a new dawn, and we are called to act on the callings we hear.

I open this section with a poem to help you visualize not just light but a lighted path, the unstable pebbles where you once trod being transformed into stepping-stones. I wrote this poem on the night Hurricane Sandy was about to make landfall in the northeastern states in year 2012.

Imagine yourself in a room full of candles, meditating and indulging in their glow and warmth. Serenity. Peace. Feel God's promise to be there by your side.

A Painter of Light

If only for one night,
Let me be a painter of light,
Illuminating your broken pathways,
Offering hope for brighter days,
Outpouring love to heal and atone,
Transforming pebble to stepping-stone.

Each brush stroke is a candlelight,
Cast to the canvas of the night.
Each candle is a lamppost,
Rooted firmly in the ground.
Let each be a guidepost
To a life that's rich and sound.
All candles are the masterpiece,
Not made by one but all.
The candles send a message.
You will rise, not fall.

Let your eyes follow the flames
As they point toward the sky.
Our master God, our maker,
Promises to be there by your side.
The flames will fade in hours,
But the memory will never die.
The art's preserved forever
In your heart and in your eyes.

The following poem reminds us of God's Spirit and our landscape growing brighter with holy light.

Spirit, Spirit Everywhere

I've come too far to give up now.
I've set my sights on more.
Greatness and rewards to come,
More than I had before.

The Spirit on my backside
Works on my behalf for sure.
What seems scary and uncertain
To God is vivid and pure.

The Spirit on my left and right
Works constantly yet out of sight.

The Spirit ahead of me,
At steps I have not taken,
Gently nudges me forward
To an outcome not mistaken.

For at those milestones to be reached,
Each awaits a welcoming marker.
The paths grow brighter with holy light
As the landscape glows where it once was darker.

Faith, Hope, and Love

Faith, hope, and love are guiding principles. Within this poetic section, I have chosen to introduce another sense. As we read black-and-white text, we use our sight. It is so important to use our ears. I can't make music play through the pages of this book, but I can remind you of songs. I invite you to play and listen to the words of the song titles I have named. You will have your favorites and may think of others. I have selected some I feel go along well with the poetic themes in this memoir.

Music is a wonderful gift. So cherish music as the child of God you are!

Amazing Grace
Because He Lives
Be Thou My Vision
Blessed Be the Name
Do, Lord, Remember Me
For the Beauty of the Earth
Here I Am, Lord
He Touched Me
How Great Thou Art
It Is Well with My Soul
Jesus Loves Me
Leaning on the Everlasting Arms
Let Us Break Bread Together
My Hope Is Built
On Eagle's Wings
Pass It On
Savior, Like a Shepherd Lead Us
Standing on the Promises
The Old Rugged Cross
There's Something About That Name
This Is My Father's World
This Little Light of Mine
'Tis So Sweet to Trust in Jesus
Victory in Jesus
What a Friend We Have in Jesus

Faith—when we have faith, we rely on God's promises.

With one simple word, faith is belief ... reliance on the promises of God.

A Path Called Belief

Wide is the gate.
Narrow is the way.
Reflect on that thought.
Watch and pray.

Visualize a bridge
With you on one side.
God stands on the other,
Wanting you to decide
To cross the bridge fully
Or take steps and retreat.
Will you reach the side
To stand next to God's feet?

He'll stand for what is right and good
In His Spirit we can't see.
He's not flesh and bones like us,
But He'll lead us to be free
Through that narrow way
That we may think is wide,
Stepping straight upon a path
To be by His great side.

Faith is belief in miracles and transformation.

The Spirit and Vine

From dawn to dusk and dusk to dawn,
God, thank You, for the light,
The warmth of the sun, the glow of the moon
That illuminates the night.
We count on light like Your promises.
You faithfully walk by our side
Every second, every minute, and each hour,
Our eternal friend and guide.
There when we struggle and when we succeed
With power to transform like vegetation from seed.
You can produce miracles and feats that we can't,
Turning impossible to possible like fruits from a plant.
Be our fruit of the Spirit,
Our vegetation on the vine.
We trust You, dear Lord,
Your will ever thine.

Trust that God will open our eyes.

Peekaboo Love

Peekaboo, you can't see Me,
But I can see you cheerfully.
Your eyes are closed.
You think I'm not here.
My news for you:
I'm close and near.
By your side,
I'm the guide.
I hold the plan
To show you can
Be who you are meant to be,
Prospering in victory
Through baby steps,
And leaps and bounds,
Higher skies,
And lower grounds.
Everywhere your eyes will cast
My love and presence meant to last.

Faith is trust in darkness when we cannot see.

What If?

What if tomorrow,
You couldn't see
And your vision
Relies on memory?
To truly live by faith, not sight,
Trust in darkness,
The ultimate blind light.

Faith is trust beyond our eyes and ears.

Faith at Work

Faith at work that I can't espy,
Naked to my eye.
Faith at work that I can't hear,
Inaudible to my ear.

Even when both eyes and ears
Are giving full attention,
God works beyond all sight and sound
By His means and convention.

He chooses.
He decides.
He supports.
He provides.

His ways and means at His disposal
Are the epitome of any proposal.

His wondrous works so demonstrate
All we have to celebrate.

Honor God and be faithful each day
So blessedness may come your way.

Exercise active faith in your own faith.

Faith in Your Faith

Put faith in your faith, not faith in your fears.
Avoid feeling miserable and drowning in tears.

Practice faith, though it you can't see.
Let it triumph over fear and just let it be.

As if you have tucked fear to rest,
Dreamed a sweet dream: "I am so blessed."

Allow faith to be active and root in your mind.
Better days are forthcoming and nights restfully kind.

Trust in what lies ahead.

He Said

It's a cool and silent night
When all the stars are shining bright.

Away to the heavens I look up high.
What's beyond that deep, dark sky?

While everyone is tucked away,
I wait for the dawn of a brand-new day.

Suddenly, before I know,
The sun has arisen. Oh, what a glow!

Tomorrow brings a smile to my face,
The warmest of memories I gladly embrace.

The season changes; the cycle turns new
Of wishes and dreams we hope do come true.

For no one knows what lies ahead,
But God is with us. "Trust me," He said.

Trust whatever God sends.

God Sends

If every day was a page in a book,
Every few days a chapter,
If every ending was a cliffhanger,
We'd eagerly follow thereafter.

If every few years were a series,
Every decade a maturing age,
We may not find a climax
On any particular page.

But that is life with its ups and downs,
Twists, turns, and bends,
Living for the unexpected
That tomorrow is whatever God sends.

Whatever puzzles you, He clarifies.

Picturesque

In life's puzzles, there is meaning
When we're deaf and blind
To God's plan unfolding
On the horizon yet to find.

Then one day the horizon once far
Is so close at hand:
Picturesque with clarity
That you understand.

The puzzle is not so puzzling.
The pieces seem to fit:
Picturesque to ears and eyes
Like a candle freshly lit.

A beautiful flame
You can touch with a finger
Lights the horizon.
Now worries don't linger.

Hope—when we have hope, we gain new perspectives and see beyond boundaries.

With two simple words, hope is just because, ... anchored deeply in the soul.

Just Because

Just because I hold hope in my mind
And faith in my heart,
Those treasures propel me
To make a fresh start,
To rise each morning
Knowing dawn will bring
Gifts and joys
Harmonious choirs do sing.
But do you hear music
In a well-lit background?
Or are you focused on priorities
In a dim foreground?
Have you gotten caught up in this world's hectic pace
That you often overlook your peripheral space?
The peripheral and the boundaries will reveal so much,
Add perspectives and views that impact and touch.
Just because I hold faith in my heart and hope in my mind,
I can keep moving forward and leave sorrows behind.

Hold on like traction in action.

Bond and Be Kind

Faith, hope, and love in action:
Three little words when I need some traction,
Traction to pull me out of the mire
When I feel stuck like I've got a flat tire.
Faith to count on when the going gets rough.
Hope to persevere when I need to get tough.
Love for my own self transcends to others.
Be kind to yourself, all sisters and brothers.
We dwell in one big community,
Serving gratefulness in spiritual unity.
Together, let's bond and hand-in-hand bind.
Love be so active; faith and hope be so kind.

Leave worries behind.

Cloudy Imagination

If a cloud were reserved for me,
Over Earth I'd tower,
Looking down on God's creation,
Sitting high with power.

As I peer up at the sky,
The clouds look soft like cotton.
Peacefully, they drift and float.
Troubles all forgotten.

The clouds so white and puffy,
Like a pillow to lay my head.
Sleep so filled with dreams,
No nightmares from my bed.

Even the clouds can look a bit scary
On days hasty and hurried,
Like a twister about to brew
As if the skies are worried.

The sky is like emotion,
Can be tormented and hazy.
Unlike a clear, sunny day,
The fog gets ever crazy.

Through the fog there starts a mist,
Refreshing in tiny drops.
Later that day the clouds release more.
The rainfall plops and plops.

I know there will come a sunny day, no cloud in the sky.
Although I cannot see you, I didn't say good-bye.

I can dream about the clouds
Forming pillows in my mind.
Imagination moves me.
My worries are left behind.

Vibrate in the present.

The Wow Is Now

To vibrate in the present,
Is to feel your breath now,
That very defining moment,
That very powerful wow.
Not dwelling in the past
Of what ifs, if only, should've.
Not worrying about the future,
Nor all the possible could've.
For the moment holds potential
That's really existential.
All those little steps now
Work to blend somehow.
Each and every step,
Moving to and fro,
Vibrating in the present,
Uncharted as you go.

Await safely in the palm of God's hand.

Keeper of Me

Whatever today demands of me,
Whatever He commands of me,
I may secretly long to do otherwise.
He sees right through any disguise.
Cannot run, cannot hide.
He's everywhere by my side,
Like my "keeper" so I don't get lost
And stray too far away,
Like my "guardian" sheltering me
So I don't drift one day.
Finding safety in the palm of His hand,
A hand so big it holds all the land.
All the oceans and skies so blue;
Keeper of my dreams and fantasies too.
And with those secrets I so share,
He knows my future and all I will fare.
As I evolve from His palm, His hand,
I anxiously await all that He has planned.

Expect tomorrow to be greater than the day before.

Tomorrow Comes a New Moon

Look at yesterday as history,
Since that is what it was.
Can't repeat a single day ago,
And this I say because:
Today is a still frame fleeting:
Here today, gone tomorrow,
A precious moment of time
You simply just can't borrow.
Face tomorrow like a new moon
Soon and very soon.
Forthcoming as the greater day
Repeatedly along the way,
Forthcoming as the greater way,
Each and every successive day.

Let your journey be a ride on a rainbow of hope shimmering with light.

Ride the Rainbow

Ride the rainbow,
Its promise, its sign,
Not just when rain pours
And the sun does shine.
Visualize a bent rainbow.
It is a beautiful arc
That illuminates the sky
And so masks the dark.
So we focus on light
Of seven vivid hues,
Shades of primary
Reds, yellows, and blues.
But behind those colors
Are promises and your ride;
To journey with God
Right by each other's side.
Ride together with hope as you go,
For a shimmering ride to brighten every shadow.

Love—when we have love, we hold tender sentiment.

With three simple words say, "I love you."

We connect faith, hope, and love as belief just because I love you.

Love is a both a choice and commitment we make. Belief stems from love and love conquers fear.

First John 4:18 says, "There is no fear in love. But perfect love drives out fear, because fear has to do with punishment. The one who fears is not made perfect in love."

The greatest commandments in the Bible are these:

Matthew 22:37 says, "Jesus replied: 'Love the Lord your God with all your heart and with all your soul and with all your mind.'"

Matthew 22:39 says, "And the second is like it: 'Love your neighbor as yourself.'"

When we share love, we brighten another's heart. Several years ago I received a special Christmas gift from my mother. It is a beautiful oval wooden frame that encircles dried flowers and the following message:

Having someplace to go is
Home.
Having someone to love is
Family.
Having both is a
Blessing.

May this blessing ring true to your heart as you think about how you bless others and how they bless you in return.

Love is sentimental.

Sentimental, Sentiment

Love wrapped in a hug,
Welcoming arms so tight,
From family and friends we love,
Precious to our sight.

When parted for days, weeks, or months,
The bond is always there
Until you meet again one day
With hugs and love to share.

There's something extra beautiful
In relationships parted for years;
And that's the faith, hope, and love
To reunite with heartfelt tears.

Years turn over many calendar pages
Of smaller time increments.
It's tough to be long departed
From loved ones holding tender sentiments.

Remember the importance of those
Distantly spaced communions.
Turn sentiment into sentimental,
Everlasting, ever-happy reunions.

We miss those we love and wait for special reunions.

Missing Is to Have

So close and yet so far away.
Did you have to go?
So far and yet so close in heart.
Can't you stay? Although—
You've been called away for God's plans and reasons,
Now everyone who loves you, faces a new season;
Adjusting to your opportunity
While time and distance part.
But only for a temporary time,
You'll return to each missing heart.

Missing is not defined by loss.
Missing means you have one;
Someone special to wait for,
Returning when the job's done.

If I were called away,
I too would want to be missed,
Knowing I have others to miss me
And that I was never dismissed
From loved ones' hearts and minds,
Who reside so far away,
Until I could make it back to them
On the season's brightest day.

Sometimes reunions take us by surprise.

Two Frogs

Two frogs sitting by a pond
Near a lily pad and frond.

Two frogs hopping far away.
Will they reunite one day?

Two frogs living on their own
Suddenly feel all alone.
One frog misses the other frog.
Will the other come out of the fog?

Out of the fog and into the light
To live by faith when there's no sight.

Two frogs hopping toward a pond
Near a lily pad and frond.

Long-lost frogs they are no more.
Eternal friendship is in store.

We feel a bonding of spirits when we love.

As Two Spirits Blend

Treat me special, treat me kind.
Happy times are ours to find.

Exploring the present for the gift that it is,
Leaving future and past to that which is His.

For God knows tomorrow as He does yesterday
And all the loving plans for the current precious day.

With a warm companion, a very best friend,
There's comfort in bonding as two spirits blend.

Our senses feel keen when we love.

The following poem has special meaning to me. I displayed it in the church entryway where I was married.

Let Me

Let me say what's in my heart.
My thoughts run deep; I must impart.
Let me hear what song I sing,
Words so sweet with passion they bring.
Let me touch with a helping hand
To feel what's real as the warmth of the sand.
Let me smell the budding rose.
Between two thorns, forever it grows.
Let me see the beauty inside.
What we have we cannot hide.
Let me love this life I live.
To make you proud, what more can I give?

My alternate version of the poem above ends with the following line:

To make you laugh, what more can I give?

Doesn't laughter make you feel so much better? And it has no price tag. It is simply like free medicine … a prescription for your soul.

As youngsters, we eyed others and played childhood games.

In the following poem, I wrote through the eyes of a young lad who secretly admires a lovely lass.

Recess Games

"Duck, duck, goose."
My heart runs on the loose.
I eye my prize
With my two eyes.

My love, my catch,
Is mine to snatch.
And when I do,
I'll sing and woo.

Then we can sleep;
Our love we'll keep.

Then by day, we shall play
Childhood games of many names;
Quote nursery rhymes,
Share giggle times.

The school bell rings.
Recess will end.
Back to my desk,
Behind my friend.

I eye her hair, so blond and fair.
I'd recognize her smile anywhere.

In my dreams, next recess is
A chasing game again,
When she says to me, "Tag. You're it,"
And I run for her to win.

Loving guidance from others leads us toward more love.

So Wise

Inspired by divine will,
The prophet led the way.
He shouted to the pilgrims,
"I will not lead you astray!
I lead you where I've already been,
But you have not been before.
I offer a great prophecy.
Behold what is in store.
You will reap divinity.
Experience the Holy Trinity.
Agape love you need,
Faith as wee as a mustard seed.
Let this journey be a quest
Of spiritual devotion and ardor,
A trek of passion and patience
As you walk cloaked in holy armor."

Open to selfless, unconditional love
While shielded by no physical disguise,
The prophet, so inspired and wise himself,
Chanted, "Fear the Lord and grow wise."

The pilgrims, so inspired,
Trusted the prophet that day.
They began to fear the Lord
And carried on in discipleship way.

Pilgrims following a prophet
Led by prophecy,
A wise prophet guiding pilgrims
To agape love and legacy.

In the previous poem, the prophet led a journey. A journey is much like an adventure. We trek to new sights and experiences.

Love embodies so much and takes the form of many meanings. Throughout the remainder of the "Be Still the Dawn" section, I refer to other dawns to express love and our love of life.

Life is a journey, one adventure after another. Life is your story. You may not journal and write your story on paper, but you live your story every single day.

Artistically speaking, life is like a painting, and you are the focal point. You decide how to author and paint your life, your canvas.

The Dawn of Adventure

Life is one big canvas.

Adventuring

Everyone has an inward canvas—
Eyes to see and have perspective,
A heart to feel and be reflective.

Everyone has an outward canvas—
To paint before alluring eyes,
To touch dear hearts with no disguise.

If life is one big canvas each day,
Live an adventure like no other way.

Your adventure may take you high and low.
Perhaps to others, you are a hero.

As we author and paint our lives,
We're all in this together,
Taking in and giving out,
Adventuring all kinds of weather.

Sail to old and new harbors.

Sailing

Life is succeeding, and life is failing.
Importantly, life is not smooth sailing.
With God as the captain and I as His mate,
God will so guide me to avoid reckless fate.
For each new marina
I sail to, dock, and don't sink
Is an adventure I've learned from
As I move brink to brink.
For each new edge
That marks a slope I have climbed
Is just the beginning of
A new opportunity well timed.
God may steer me back to some harbors,
Challenging my navigation skill.
All those wonderful sailing lessons
This mate has learned with will.

Find a new passage; open a new door.

Passage Anew

Don't let the dawn fade away.
Each morning brings a brand-new day.
No day is like the day before.
Time to open an unknown door.
One door may have closed
Right before your eyes.
New doors are available.
A word to the wise:
If you get caught up in what might have been,
Your head will ache and mourn and spin.
Reach out and turn a brand-new key.
If the door doesn't open,
Then knock; you will see
A fresh chapter, a new verse
Awaiting through the entryway—
The passage anew that takes you through
The open, inviting doorway.

Pioneer and venture to new heights.

A Pioneer, a Pearl

Where have I been?
How did I get here?
Started inland, arrived at the bay.
Am I an explorative pioneer?

If you've trailblazed and ventured,
Taken charge of your life,
Commanded "your very ways,"
Then like an early settler
Who cleared new land,
You've pioneered "your days."

Perhaps you've innovated,
Renovated,
Implemented change,
Climbed to new heights,
Been a go-getter,
Explored a vast, new range.

Gone for the distance
They call the long haul.
Seized opportunities
Before they befall.

Then I would call you a pioneer,
An adventurer in your own right.
The world is your oyster—don't be surprised.
A pearl may unveil in sight.

The Dawn of the Seasons and Nature

Your moments and adventures move you forward in time. You witness many changes in your surroundings. Be guided by God's protection and safe harbor.

Seasons Change and Pass

Up the creek without a paddle,
Feeling lost ashore.
God, provide me a safe harbor.
Open up a door.

The open door reminds me
Of the door that closed behind me.
Passing through without a key,
Gliding quite invisibly.

As the seasons change,
It all seems oh so strange.

As the seasons pass,
I inhale new breath of life.
Yet I can count on cycles,
Uphill wins, and downhill strife.

Life is full of up-the-creek moments,
Secure times, and some fear.
But pray for harbors and open doors
As God protects you year by year.

Witness nature's patterns and cycles.

Message of the Trees

The rhythm of four cyclical seasons—
Winter, spring, summer, and fall.
Amazingly gaze and observe the trees.
Their life pattern says it all.
Barren trees turn to leafy-filled branches,
And back again we learn
The message of change over time
As the calendar's pages do turn.

Step into the trees and gaze from the inside out.

Inside God's Trees

I love moderate winds with just enough gust
To set branches in motion and hurl a good thrust.
The back-and-forth motion resembles a greeting,
Like waving our hands to initiate a meeting.
My favorite is palm fronds so long and so wide.
They cast great honor as hailed side by side.
I love weeping willows that flow like fountains,
As they blow in the wind like sheltering mountains.
They remind me of being a young girl running under
When I looked inside out with a gaze full of wonder.

Step into a garden for solace and peace.

Seek Solace

Seek solace in the garden
When you feel your heart harden
With questions and doubts,
Guilt or misgiving.
Ask yourself frankly,
"How is it I'm living?"
Soft and pure? Smothered and needy?
Insecure? Selfish and greedy?

Live softly and purely,
Like freshly watered vines,
Stemming from the garden,
Where each vine entwines.
The dewdrops speak nurture.
The dewdrops just speak,
Clinging to the greens
At each leaf's pointy peak.
When you hold out your hand
To catch the water so fine,
Let it feel like baptism
From each dropping vine,
Giving you comfort,
Such unspeakable peace,
From a network of vines
That let dewdrops release.

Stare at the vivid sky and dream of endless possibilities.

Vivid and Endless

The canvas in the sky
Is the vastest work of art,
Leading our eyes to look above
Where fields and waters part.

There is such defined seam
Between waters and the lands,
Where blue joins greens and browns
By such beautiful color bands.

But do you see the vividness in the sky so high
When a rainbow doesn't paint, and the weather is so dry?

It doesn't take sunshine and rain,
Sent by God above,
To see that across the sky,
It's painted with His love.

The sky may look so solid blue,
Be streaked with a spectrum of unimaginable hue.
The sky may be dotted with clouds so white,
Smiling at us, radiant and bright.

The sky is not meant to be bounded by seams
But to be endless much like our dreams.

For as you stare at the vivid sky
With all your wants and needs,
Dream of those possibilities
The endless sky so feeds.

Visualize scenes we've yet to fully see.

Yet Unseen

Rainbow violet
To rainbow red.
Inside out.
Remember, He said.

It's a sign
Only He can provide.
It's a message
So far and so wide.

Though we may seek
To find the arc's end,
That's impossible.
It's God's glorious bend
That appears when He paints the sky,
Briefly hello and then fading good-bye.

But He returns to paint again
The most vivid, majestic scene
To remind us of His promises
Our eyes have not yet seen.

Catch yourself so awesomely amazed.

Amazed in Awe

Something unusual,
Something rare.
It caught my eye.
It made me stare.

The sky turned orange,
Then hazed with pink.
Amazed in awe,
I sure did think.

Find nature's beauty in our high-tech highway maze.

Highway Maze

I saw endless fields in my childhood days,
A bountiful crop the Indians called "maize."

The country flowed with crop after crop,
Wondering if I'd spy a boundary to drop.

Drop and turn into new kinds of fields
Where highways take over producing fast yields.

It's there I saw where country became city,
Fast paced and mad raced, a rapid-sung ditty.

As if cars were growing instead of tall corn,
Like a race against time with each blowing horn.

Honks replaced frogs, crickets, and nature's fine sounds.
Tall buildings towered upward from man's bounded grounds.

Bounded where man cleared the land and paved ways
For future generations and high-tech driven days.

Where does the high-tech boundary drop?
Are there any fields left to harvest a crop?

Listen for nature: those frogs and those crickets
In the countryside, in the green, grassy thickets.

They've not disappeared in these newer, present days,
But they're harder to find in this world's highway maze.

The Dawn of Hearing a Higher Call

At a silent time, you hear a whisper ... calling you by name.

Serene by the Sea

The serene sea
I serenely see.

The empty bench
Along the way,
Where no one sits
Along the bay.
The wooden bench is deeply sketched—
"All things are possible with God"—so etched.

Does everyone fear to sit on its wood?
This I have not understood.

The pedestrians and bikers pass it by,
Choosing some other seat under the sky.

Where they too serenely see,
The serene sea just like me.

But today I choose to occupy
That lonely bench ahead I eye.

I sit right down under weeping willows
And watch the crests of rolling sea billows.

I invite them to flow upon my feet.
Today, I occupy the mercy seat.

It called my name, so I came.

It may be wood, but it looked gold,
Like the Ark of the Covenant, I am told.

Inside, I feel so serene,
Lavishing the seaside scene.

This is a call of reassurance.

His Higher Call

Believe in God's Word.
Trust in His ways.
Follow His guidance
Forever, always.
Live His commandments
Not one day but all.
Seek reassurance
From His higher call.
His promises are great.
His promises are true.
Heaven awaits
For me and for you.

This is a calling so ever gentle.

Until

When a higher call is calling you,
Slow down, be still.
Don't miss the gentle message
Echoing His will … until.
You may have followed your ambitions,
Your will … until.
Until fleeting moments stopped;
Echoing slow down, be still.
Until now, life seemed so fast.
All those footsteps of your past.
All that history to this day
Paved a walk along the way.
Walking close with God or veering,
Understand that He is steering.
Until you heard His call,
You may have feared a hardened fall.
Until you released the wheel,
Faith may not have felt so real.
But now with faith and hope,
His will be your guide.
Your walk will feel so gentle,
Footsteps pacing side by side.

This is a calling that says to let go and let God.

The Bones Do Hear

If the Spirit says sing,
Let your voice so ring.
Shine, Jesus, shine.
Let the heavens be mine!
If the Spirit says dance,
Let your feet carry you away.
With so much heart and soul,
You feel swept by joy today.
If the Spirit says, "Step out
Away from your comfort zone,"
Then shift your body out
To the realm of the unknown.
If the Spirit says, "Let go of a crutch"
For His assurance beyond what you clutch,
Then let go and let God lead you.
He is there to comfort. He will feed you.
For He has sent the Lamb of God,
Sufficient for us to atone,
To have eternal life in our Lord
And a joyful heart without a dry bone.

Transcend yourself higher, fuller, and deeper.

Transcend beyond the Ego

Star so bright that catches my sight,
Let me wish upon this night
For joys that outnumber piercing pains,
For victories during woes and rains,
For turnarounds when life so plummets,
For uphill climbs to reach the summits,
For the summit is a glorious view
To scan the horizon of every hue;
From fields of gold, bronze, and brown
To skies of blue like a royal crown.
At that moment, I'm freed from my ego
And transcend so fully and deeply
To a higher self I've sought
And wished for very secretly.

This is a calling we call "grace."

Our Saving Grace

Where there is grace, there is God!

God
Reflecting
    our
Attitudes
    toward the
Cross
    and what it
Embodies.

God
Revealing
    His
Almighty
Character
    and
Excellence.

God
Reaching
Around
    His
Cherished
Earth.

God
Responding
    and
Answering
    His
Children's
Echoes.

Where there is God, there is grace.

The Dawn of Expressing Praise

Where there is grace, there is praise ... with the spirit and harmony of devotion and evangelism.

Peace

Let the epicenter be prayer,
Practiced daily and everywhere.
Everywhere let evangelism flow.
All footsteps that we tarry and go.
Go out in the spirit of giving alms,
With devotion to the Word and Psalms.
Psalms, ringing in blissful communion,
By people singing blessings in peaceful reunion.
Peace so wonderful and gloriously everlasting;
Heart of our desires, eternal and lasting.

Show glory through voicing.

To Glorify

God so worthy and majestic
In a royal robe,
Standing tall with mystery
Vaster than the largest globe.
I picture you elevated
Like a statue with great height.
But a statue you will never be.
You move with endless might.
You make miracles happen.
You're alive and not made of stone.
Yet you are a solid rock,
The firmament of life's throne.
Your throne is everywhere,
Yet the statue needs its base.
The statue has no mobility.
It's stone from toes to face.
Let us not be statues
When there are messages to be spread.
God, Your people who glorify You
Shall voice what we've heard and read.

216

Speak glory through Scripture.

Script to Scripture

Remind me daily.
Life's more than a script.
Life's short as it is.
We speak, and we lip.
From our mouths
We must take care,
To leave unsaid
The unkind and unfair,
To speak as if we've moved from script to Scripture
And paint so vividly a warmhearted picture.
A picture not cryptic,
But visibly plain;
Accepting human nature,
All sunshine and rain.

Show glory through song and dance.

Sing and Dance

And they all said, "Awake in the morning.
There's glory in the sky."
And they all said, "Sing in the morning.
The Lord wants you to try."

And they all said, "Dance in the afternoon,
Beneath the sun's bright light."
And they all shouted in the afternoon,
"Keep it up till night."

So they sang and danced while the sun set
As the moon rose ever high.
They sang, and they danced in the moonlight
That brightened star-filled sky.

They said, "Amen" and "Good night."
Sweet dreams; sleep so tight.

The buttercups will dance in the morn.
The birds will soar and sing high.
The songs and dance in your heart
Will be the apple of your eye.

Show praise through any musical style you choose.

Lord of Dance and Song

The guitar's strum,
The beat of the drum,
The chime of the bell
All sound so swell.
The horn's toot,
The tone of the flute,
The clang of the cymbal
All sound so nimble.
Brass, percussion, wind, and string
Harmonize an orchestral zing.
Country and rock,
Folk and rap blare,
Opera and jazz,
Oldies and new wave on the air.
Blues, gospel, a bit of hip-hop.
Could swing and reggae be your bebop?
Whatever musical liking flows you along,
Let the Lord be your dance and your favorite song.

The Dawn of Communion with Jesus

We praise our friend Jesus.

John 15:13 says, "Greater love has no one than this: to lay down one's life for one's friends."

He is ... the rosebud, the rose.

The Scallop, the Weed, and the Rosebud

Scallop with me, fishermen,
Who gather at the shore.
Harvest, O bountiful harvest,
From depths of seabed floor.

Weed with me, O gardeners,
Who congregate in fields.
Throw away the undesirable
To multiply the yields.

Bloom, O tiny rosebud,
And grow like no beauty before,
For I've got my eyes on you,
The one I so adore.

Jesus may be a rosebud to you
As you remember His birth in a manger.
Harvest His love; garden with Him.
He'll never be a stranger.

Scallop holy words.
Weed out sinful flavor.
Soak in the spirit of the "rose"
As it grows with wisdom and favor.

Scallop for kind fellowship.
Weed out troublesome annoyances.
Cultivate communion with the "rose"
And bloom in abundant joyances.

He is beautiful beyond compare.

If Jesus Were a Rose

The bud is blooming,
Soon to be a rose.
Unfolding every petal,
Beautifully grows.

Unlike any other rose,
It has no single thorn.
It's perfect in the sunlight
From the dawning morn.

Just one thing about the rose;
No flower can compare.
The rose outshines them all.
Its beauty is so rare.

He is the Bread and the Wine.

Come to the Table

Oh holy table of oaks, pines, and maples.
Come kneel before, partake of the staples.

The Bread we call the staff of life;
Remember Christ's body broken in strife.

The Wine, His blood shed for you and for me,
Reflects salvation for mankind to feel free.

To not feel hungry or thirsty or dry
But to demand so much of the adequate supply.

A supply that won't run out and deplete.
Come to the table for a sacrament seat.

He is the one true Light.

Light, Shine Down

Light of the World, the one true Light,
Carry me through hours of day and night.

When sun and moon seem pale to me,
Reveal Your loving Spirit to me.

Whether I see it in stars or a garden,
Do not let my heart so harden.

Open my heart and my tear-stricken eyes
To the majestic heaven and Your works from the skies.

Light of the World, shine down on me.
Bless me with care so lovingly.

Be the light that shines on me.

Shine on Me

Shine on me; I'll radiate.
The glow will not grow dim,
A glow so bright and lustrous,
Melodious as a hymn.

Be the light that reflects God-given dignity.

The Living Christ Within

As we discover the living Christ in you and me,
We realize self-love and feel ever free.

Not trapped by what others would have us be
But taking our stance in society.

Standing on our spiritual terms,
Not measured high or low;
Not even comparing our standards
To those of friend or foe.

For we have found a comfort
Driven from Christ within,
Possessing a realization
That He died for our sin.

We understand we are commanded
To love one another.
We're all made in God's image,
Every sister and every brother.

Deep within woman and man
Dwells God-given dignity
To respect ourselves and others
As God would so want us to be.

For the living Christ within
Outshines our dark shadows with His Light.
His beauty makes us beautiful.
Christ is our true inner Light.

The Dawn of Treasuring Friendships

This section is devoted to the special relationship of friendship. I introduce it with a Bible verse that inspired me to write the opening poem.

Proverbs 27:6 says, "Wounds from a friend can be trusted, but an enemy multiplies kisses."

Think about bread. It is a sustainer. We call Jesus the "Sustainer of Life," and when partaking in communion, we break bread to symbolize His body broken for us. Jesus is the Bread of Life.

As you read this section, be reminded, "To need a friend is to knead a friend."

Baking bread takes time. Relationships require patience and time as if character traits of people start acting like yeast that eventually leavens. Your friendships become transformed for the better. They become invaluable, and you treasure them.

Friends are virtuous.

Friendship Bread

A good friend brings us joy and often heartache.
Sometimes sadness we feel is more than we can take,
For if we hurt a friend, then we hurt more than the other,
As if we've bonded to feel pain, as one spirit we discover.

"Friendship is a single soul dwelling in two bodies," as Aristotle so said.
He wisely took these words as yeast and sowed and left us bread,
For these words are really food for the soul and digestion for the heart.
A friendship of virtue is the highest, long lasting, and set apart,
From many other relationships that fleetingly pass by,
That drift like clouds and move on to some other changing sky.
For friends of virtue dance under one consistent sky;
They see inside each other's hearts and never say good-bye.

They feel the other's pain as if it were their own,
But to lose the other one feels like a wounded bone.

Friends are extensions of each other.

As We

Friend, I turn to you for great light
When it's dim and not feeling right.
Perhaps you'll utter just the right word
When wrong words before are what I so heard.
Perhaps you'll touch when I need help dearly,
Sensing and hearing my needs oh so clearly.
Whatever the word, whatever the touch,
Your presence I treasure and can ne'er be too much.
Friend, my arm, an extension of me,
I appreciate your support that defines us as "we."

Friends show loyalty and acceptance.

To Be Pals

It's okay to be my pal, my comrade, and my friend,
Walking with each other around each turn and bend.

Showing loyalty, deep and true,
Reserved for just a chosen few.

Who accept me as I be,
A special bond with you and me.

When we're up, when we're down.
When we smile, when we frown.

Who gives things time as if time were endless,
To not lose out and feel so friendless.

Yet who treasures all the pleasure,
Suffers when the other feels pain;
And feels pain that one has caused,
Bearing down such strain.

For hurt runs in feelings and thoughts,
But happiness sure does too;
So, my pal, my comrade, my friend,
I'm happy to be with you.

Friends laugh together.

To Laugh Each Day

From fields of blue bonnets,
May you hear beautiful sonnets.
Below willows that weep,
May they lull you to sleep.
'Neath the rays of the sun,
May you run and have fun.
'Neath the rising moon,
May your laughter come soon.
If you've spent hours during any long day
Without a dose of notable laughter,
Before you pull down the nighttime shades,
Ne'er forget daily humor is prescribed hereafter.

Friends complement one another and sense belonging.

Peas and Carrots

That night I was an orange carrot,
A vegetable in my mind;
I rose from my bed to quietly creep
For a veggie like in kind.

I crept and scurried like a mouse,
Seeking a spirit in my house.
Perhaps a friend like two peas in a pod.
No, that's not right, as this carrot did nod.
I'm not a mouse, so I don't seek cheese.
Who am I seeking as I crawl on my knees?
I'm not a cat seeking a mouse.
Can I find the veggie in my house?

I approached the telephone
With feelings so persistent.
Then a calling was so answered
For friendship so consistent.
A friend to complement this carrot
When some veggies just don't pair;
A friend like a plate of green peas
That goes together beyond compare.

Memories say, "I care."

Finding the Way

Sometimes we are led astray
On a cold and cloudy day.
What we feel and what we know
Might not tell us where to go.

So take time to understand
The problem that is at your hand.
The solution might not come today,
But light will surely show the way.

When you know that others care,
All problems you can somehow bear.
That warm and sunny way you'll find,
When you leave your doubts behind.

Care flows in circles and two-way trends
When you stand among true friends;
Who bond with memories of fondness and care;
Who support God's will for the life you do share.

Gestures say, "I care."

Surely 'Tis

Is someone being friendly to you,
Even like no others compare?
Yet you are the one who may resist
When no threat is ever there?

Has someone invited you into his or her life
And opened up to share
A multitude of words
That sum up one word, *care*?

Maybe you need to tell that friend
How valued the friendship is
And that you never want to lose
A bond that surely 'tis.

Longing for shared moments says, "I miss you."

Biding Time Is Biting Time

I will make my moments count.
They're not tasks I'm obligated to do.
Tasks can be postponed,
Not like a moment spent with you.

For you are here today.
Who knows what tomorrow will bring?
When you are swept away
To a new song you may sing.

A new song, a new path,
A better choice you feel;
Bypassing time with me
And a moment that could've been real.

But if I really matter
Somewhere deep within your heart,
We will sing together
And know that love does ne'er depart.

For moments pass, as I have learned,
And turn into time spent waiting,
When we could've shared some time before
Without the hesitating.

They say if it's meant to be, it will,
But time doesn't stop and wait until
A new moment, a new chance.
Time is filled with circumstance.

Ticking away minutes, then hours;
What once were buds now are flowers.

What once were seeds now are trees,
And children grew taller than our knees.

As if we blinked when we were young;
And now matured, and time has stung.

Snuck up and bit us hard somewhere
As years have passed beyond compare.

And we may pine for the good ol' days
When the years ahead were more numbered.
But now past years have multiplied,
As if we've slept and slumbered.

So this day called "today."
I wake, counting on a moment with you
Before no time remains for us
As future shrinks; how true.

Friends touch and form bonds.

Friendship Prints

Friends touch each other with fingerprints,
Loving stamps, and little hints.

Tiny cues that do imprint,
Impressing hearts with colorful tint.

Friends paint colors that blend forever,
Bonding relationships that do not sever.

Let us marvel at those fingerprints.
Walk together in companion blueprints.

For our friendship photographs
Show all our prints from fingers to toes,
Our loving, cherished memories
And emotional expressions we expose.

Friends seek and value each other dearly.

Glisten

To glisten is to shine like a star that won't burn out,
To show your true luster from the soul inwardly out.

To glisten like a gem, radiant as a sapphire,
Let integrity be your strength that others so admire.

Listen to your conscience, what your inner jewel does say,
Encouraging you to do right and not feel led astray.

You are a jewel, a much-cherished gem,
Valued by God and certainly all of them—
Those who are true friends,
Those who seek you out,
For if you were lost like a coin,
They'd search all around and about.

All friends together
Hold your gems so near,
Like shiny coins that glisten
And you value oh so dear.

Friends are blessings who dream together.

Old Friends

May your paths converge to greet you
When time has been long and passed.
May you walk with old friends dearly,
Cherishing memories that will always last.

When paths take you far away,
Dream of future times together
As friends who've cemented such a bond
That survives all trials and weather.

Special friends feel that guardian angels look out for them.

Friends 'Neath a Halo

Friendly footprints cannot be erased
Like the blowing of the sands.
Friends create the deepest markers
As they walk with entwined hands.

Their hands don't need to physically touch.
They love each other oh so much.

It's that sensation that they feel
As two hearts seem to blush
With a warmth and deep comfort
'Neath the light of a halo's flush.

Could an angel look out for friends
And each step they take?
Could an angel be a third party
To help mark footprints they do make?

The Dawn of Angels

Angels hail peace … inviting us to see with eyes of grace.

Eyes of Grace

If I could make angels anywhere
With my mind and hands,
I'd give them wings and halos
And let them join the bands.
Bands with drums and trumpets,
Triangles, saxes, and harps,
Flutes, violins, and oboes
That harmonize all flats and sharps.
I'd cheer the bands as the angels gaze
From overhead, their voices raise,
Melodious with every tune,
Harmonious, peace comes soon,
Hailing the Prince of Peace, who raises His arms to save;
He forgives sins of believers; extends His arms to wave,
Motioning, "Come, follow Me."
The Prince of Peace will lead.
Closely behind His footsteps,
The angels and bands proceed,
Satisfying all desires, taking care of every need;
Angels, let us watch you with eyes of grace, not greed.

Angels comfort us as we rest, watching over our beds.

Angel, Angel

Sleepyhead, sleepyhead,
Angel watching over your bed.
With shining eyes that never close,
She's ever present as you doze.
Invisible to your very eye,
She's a treasure from the sky.
Her wings can take her anywhere,
But rest assured, she's everywhere.
Angel, angel overhead,
A comfort as you rest in bed.

The Dawn of Places We Call Home and Treasured Family

Home is where the heart is ... at home with loving ties.

Lovingly Dressed

My feet may leave my home, then return,
For home is in my heart as I yearn.

My feet will never walk away
From those I love each day and day.

To reach home by any means or mode,
I long for mother's warm abode.

A warmth in caring, warmth in sharing,
Oh so beautifully rich;
From years and years of memories
Bound in loving stitch.

Home—where all are remembered,
In loving ties be so tendered.

Through ups and downs,
Smiles and frowns,
Family love always rebounds.

You give love away,
And it comes right back,
Even when it seems
It fell through a crack.

A little hole that absorbed some friction,
Often the result of misguided diction.

But words are words, and actions do cure,
Keeping family and friends ever so pure.

Sparkling and fresh,
The pure in heart are so blessed,
Who through means and modes
Travel lovingly dressed.

Honor Mother.

Mother

Mother sows a family tree
As we sew a quilt you see.

All members of the family
Sharing joys and memory.

Mother hears the woes and glories
As we utter all our stories.

Mother sees our triumphs and falls,
Always there to take our phone calls.

Mother listens, doesn't tune us out;
Has patience even when we shout.

Mother senses when something is wrong,
Lends support to guide us along.

Even when she's out of sight,
She's never out of mind.
Mother is symbolic of love,
Patient and so kind.

Privately,
She's laughed and cried with me,
The matriarch of our family.

Walked me down my wedding aisle.
Journeyed with me mile after mile.

Even when something was a challenge for her,
She sacrificed time to show we were
Fine in how we handled each test;
Doing what we can, our very best.

So Mother, sew a quilt for us,
The generations ahead;
Members of the family tree
Bonded with each thread.

Mom shines day and night.

The Busy Mom

Ah, the busy mom
Seeks the right song
To right every wrong.
Ah, how we look to Mom,
As if she can coast with angel wings,
Multitask, and do wonderful things.

Manage the schedule and varied demands.
Extend support with two open hands.

Get everyone up on time.
Dance through each day in rhythm and rhyme.

Be busy and not let herself slip.
Be willing and ready for some new grand trip.

Be organized when order is desired.
And seems no one notices, she could be tired.

A busy mom has a way to keep her composure,
Getting things done and bringing closure
To a task while the next one awaits.
"Busy" describes Mom; we hear no debates.

Ah, the busy mom
As productive as you are.
You shine day and night
Like yellow sun and star.

Have fun with Father.

Knock Knock with Dad

Knock knock with a shrug.
Who's there? It's Hug.
Hug who?
Hug you.

Knock knock a lot.
Who's there? It's Got.
Got who?
Got you.

Knock knock no fad.
Who's there? It's bad.
Bad who?
Bad too.

"No way," I say.
"You silly, Dad.
We're all good
And no way bad."

For you are just a teddy bear,
Whom I squeeze to show I care.
Then you pat me, and you say
Loving words to me each day.

Loving pats I'll knock right back.
You will answer; that's your knack.

Great big hugs
You always share.
I would say,
"Dad, you are rare."

Glowing in my very sight,
I esteem you strong with might.
Yet tender and so very kind,
Let's knock knock if you don't mind.
Each and every day I say,
With loving hands to knock our way.

Bless children and tuck them in at night.

Miles of Rainbows

I tuck you in, O little one.
Have peace as you sleep at night.
Sweet dreams will lull your spirit
Till morning beams so bright.

After rain comes sunshine.
After tears come smiles.
Rain and sun cast rainbows.
Promises bridge smiles.

O little one off drifting,
You've many miles ahead.
The future holds miles of rainbows.
I promise you, sleepyhead.

Miss children and be overjoyed when they return home.

Missing You

Little one, not so little now,
Away just for a few days,
Momma feels the heartache.
"Come home soon," she prays.

The minutes feel like hours.
The hours feel like days.
But soon she'll be overjoyed
In the company of your ways.

For there's no smile or any hug
Just like yours alone.
Little one, not so little now,
Her son she calls her own.

The Dawn of Celebrations

Treasured family and friends draw close for weddings.

Shower with Loving Power

Happiness held is the seed.
Happiness shared is the flower.
I read this anonymous quote one day,
Thinking next what I'd write and say.
Something borrowed, something blue,
Something old, and something new.
To hold something is a treasure,
But to share something is a dear pleasure.

A seed can't be just held in your hand.
It needs to be shared to grow in the land.
To give to another on a fine day,
A flower stemmed from a gifted bouquet.

Let's be reminded of a long-standing tradition,
Much like the bride tends to her wedding dress,
Making sure she's covered all "somethings"
And doesn't walk down the aisle with less.

Perhaps a new penny in her shoe,
A blue garter above her knee,
A piece of grandmother's jewelry
Displayed with great antiquity.
But if you're not looking closely enough,
You miss the important parts.
A tradition held, a tradition shared,
Transmitted between deep hearts.

A tradition held seeding happiness,
A tradition flowers share,
Uniting generations of loved ones
In something special to adorn and wear.
The giver of tradition
Wears the happiness of a beautiful flower.
The accepter of tradition
Borrows a gift adorned in loving power.

Treasured family and friends celebrate birthdays.

Birthday Wishes

Once a year a birthday comes;
A reminder of our birth.
Celebrate the honor.
Feast the glee and mirth.
If you have a cake and candles,
Close your eyes and blow.
Don't forget to make a wish,
Enriched by candle glow.
A wish is like a hope,
A prayer in your heart,
Beloved and very special,
Endearing from its start.

Treasured family and friends rejoice at Christmas.

Christmas Wishes

It's Christmastide; O what a wonderful season
To send greetings for a very special reason.

We celebrate the birth of a Son,
The One we call Jesus, our Lord Holy One.

It's a time to rejoice and a time to sing
Songs of blessings the new year will bring.

The flame of a candle that burns through the night
Inspires a message for loved one's delight
To remind us of special memories we hold
Of past Christmas stories we've long ago told.

So gather 'round the tree so bright
'Neath all the presents of red, green, and white.

Share a gift that's sent down from above
To wish every heart lots of peace, joy, and love.

Treasured family and friends shows thanks and feel blessed at Thanksgiving.

Cornucopia

All the threads so beautifully sewn
Transform to a covering lovingly homegrown,
With a local touch of the domestic homeland,
Stitched by dear women hand and hand.

With ripened vegetables and beautiful fruits
In woven baskets in fields of green shoots.

Picturesque with cornucopia,
Overflowing with flowers and corn;
Amazing bounty and abundance
Stemmed from the shape of a goat's horn.

The tapestry of the autumn season,
Known as the spring when every leaf is a flower,
Depicts harvest in vibrant colors
As if nurtured by a tender fall shower.

Most wonderfully, the harvest time
Is a reaping we celebrate once a year,
Seated at a Thanksgiving table
With loves ones drawn so near.

"Harvest time,"
Surrounded by bread;
"Reaping time,"
Blessings not left unsaid.

Thank-yous and amens,
The Bread of Life sustains
At the table so bountiful
Set with fine wheats and grains.

The Dawn of Traditions

Think about your special customs and what brings you joy. I place a single red rosebud in a vase each Christmas Eve. I enjoy its bloom as it carries me to a new year.

Find new ways to share and honor.

Gramma's Patches

She went to the attic and found a trunk
Covered with dust and scratches.
She pried the lock, peeked inside, and counted eighty-nine patches.

The initials on the trunk were her Gramma's indeed.
She pondered for a moment, *What purpose do these feed?*

As she pondered longer,
The solution shaped in her mind.
Each patch was a year of Gramma's life,
Quilt fragments that she ne'er did bind.

The patches were not sewn. The quilt was never made.
Gramma didn't see ninety; to rest at eighty-nine, she was laid.

The granddaughter decided to sew the patches but couldn't weave a ten-by-nine.
She'd make a rectangle with eighty-eight, and that is how they'd align.

She stitched the quilt for Gramma's life and saved the eighty-ninth square
To pass it down to the next generation,
A tradition for them to share.

Pass down memories.

The Hand-Me-Down Rocker

The hand-me-down rocker is not empty.
It holds priceless memories
From ancestors who rocked and nestled babes
And whispered many sweet dreams.

Look at the rocker more closely.
It looks still but is meant to rock,
To sway in back-and-forth motion.
Restore dreams and so unlock
Those deep treasures in your mind
That you discover as you meditate,
Actions that you wish to pursue
Without idleness and wait.

The rocker is idle if you see it that way.
Imagine it on its own swaying.
Meditate very deeply
About the messages it is conveying.

Our ancestors before us
Dreamed to see future generations living good,
To pass down hand-me-down messages
From a full rocker that means more than its wood.

Find meaning and comfort in the intangible.

The Front Yard Swing

The front yard swing hangs empty and bare.
At lonely times
I seek it ...
Swing softly, and I stare.

Gaze out at the lawn as the dusk closes the day,
Eyeing the sunset over low tides of bay.

They say tomorrow is a new beginning.
So is yesterday just an old ending?
"And what about today?" I do ask.
What message is this day sending?

As I swing gently back and forth,
The days I do rank in my mind.
Some have had such impact and meaning.
Others are faded and long left behind.

It is ironic how the motion of the swing
Causes me to meditate as I sway.
...Gently back in time
....
gently pushing ahead....
Or simply being still in the present day.

I can't swing on and on and on,
As soon I must stop and be still.
Just like the day I call "today,"
It has its purpose and its will.

As I leave the swing again
Empty and bare for a while,
Another lonely day will come,
And I can swing mile for mile.

243

The Dawn of Your Growth and Spiritual Maturity

Experiencing meaning and comfort in yourself is like taking root. It's a time to reap with God ... a rooted experience.

One Blade

One direction through God
Like one blade destined to bear fruit;
The earth produces by itself
From the soul-sustaining root.

Being rooted in God, like the blade that starts to grow,
Develops your spiritual soul daily so you will fully show
A sensitive attitude, a freshened maturity,
A ripened gratitude, spiritual purity.

Harvest time is when you reap from the Spirit,
For you sowed to the Spirit as you rooted,
Believing in the growth of one blade
And future promises ever well suited.

This is a blossoming experience.

A Blossoming of Grace

Let me blossom at a natural pace
As my buds unfold the growth I embrace,
Opening slowly to feel sunshine,
Catching raindrops petal to vine,
Beaming forth like a ballerina from the pistil so slender,
Dancing and spinning in harmony: ever so sweet, so tender.

A vision of loveliness, a vision of grace;
If ever was a flaw, I see no trace.

The blossom is a beauty, a sight to behold.
It naturally evolved as each petal did unfold.

This is a life-changing experience.

The Changing Frame

Let me blossom.
Don't let me wilt.
I have potential.
My frame is built.

When I am dry
Like a thirsty flower,
Nurture me
Like a thunderous shower.

Give me a challenge.
Incent me some more.
I have potential
To face what's in store:
Future steps and unknown paths,
Crossroads I'll tread one day;
Though I'll frame new memories,
The old don't fade away.

My frame is ever changing
As I blossom bud by bud,
But even a thirsty flower
Drops petals in the mud.

I won't forget those petals,
For life as I know my frame
Simply means I move forward
And don't remain the same.

This is a satisfying experience. The following poem reflects personal transition from feeling powerless to powerful and renewed.

True to Satisfaction

Powerless,
Watching and waiting,
Defenseless,
Anticipating.

Standing tall, not cowering,
In a stance
Empowering,

Others' footsteps hollow
My purpose.
Watch me follow.

A fulfillment ride beyond compare,
A satisfaction stride if I dare
To risk losing
Beyond my choosing,
To seek gain
Despite all pain,
Protected by faith and not by sight,
By a presence with glorified might.

Powerful.
I watched and waited,
In simple terms,
Emancipated,
Mounted with wings
As the eagles fly,
Renewed with strength
To more than get by.

This is a purposeful experience.

How I Impact

Things work together for the good.
Life's Ws numbered by five,
So answering these five questions
Helps us feel more spiritually alive.

Purpose in life is something we all seek.
Call it our personal design—
Who, what, when, where, and why.
The five Ws down the line.

If you were to take time
To write answers to each,
How you replied to the Ws
Surely will teach.

How you look at how your life does impact
Makes a difference as you daily interact.

But daily interaction must also include
Fellowship with God, important to exude.

For your total makeup that you do see
Is observed by others so true.
Remember to set and lead by example
As others define their Ws too.

For in the end, we all need to say,
"My life matters with purpose each day!"

As I wrote the preceding poem, I recalled my high school graduating class motto by Ralph Waldo Emerson: "What lies behind us and what lies before us are tiny matters compared to what lies within us."

When we remove the time dimension and not think about any given day, we can then answer how. We will act with purpose and strive to live life. We will draw from who we are within to answer our five Ws of life.

In the year I graduated high school, I was the class valedictorian. My topic for my speech was "What Lies Within Us." I have kept my speech all these years, and I share a few unmodified excerpts in hopes that you make a connection to my earlier comments about God leading us to the wilderness. Let this speak to you about growth and choices.

- This evening graduation sets the stage, and as the curtain rises, we are all prepared to perform. But where are the lights and cameras? We never even see this mysterious curtain that seems to divide our lives into childhood, adolescence, and adulthood.
- We have no writers to prepare a screenplay or prompters to provide us with cue cards.
- If we didn't enjoy our chosen experiences, we often edited them from our roles.
- We will never leave our role as student behind but continue to encounter learning experiences. We have all stumbled with our lines. We will find that our mistakes won't be as easy to correct as rubbing the eraser on the end of a pencil across paper.
- Reflections from our pasts enable us to be responsible today to model our lives toward our images of the challenging tomorrow we are about to enter.
- As we depart, a new curtain will rise as we will strive to fulfill our hopes, dreams, and expectations.

Now that it is years later, I add new reflection and insight:

You will walk on many pebbles before you find your seashells.

The Dawn of Your Personal Light and the Radiance You Give Yourself and Others

Walk comfortably in your shoes, … feeling first and foremost that "you" is truer than true.

Possessively You

Be you-er than you,
Truer than true,
For no one else
Can fill your shoes.
God gave you feet from which to stand
As you walk across His mighty land.
From rocks to sand,
Mountains to shores,
All those steps are possessively yours.
You may walk out of your shoes with feet bare,
But only you feel the pressure that's there.
So when you're tempted to act like another,
Remember that act is an action of smother,
Stifling yourself and your truer than true,
Obscuring yourself and your you-er than you.

Feel thankful.

Brightly Shining

If I could have one night to shine
As the brightest star in the sky,
I'd stand tall and smile so wide
As I hold my head very high.
I'd feel complete and satisfied.
I'd be so thankful and gratified.
I'd thank the Lord for such a blessing,
Truths from my mouth for full confessing.
Perhaps I'd be caught up in awe.
Perhaps I'd pray, "Don't let me fall."
But when I shine,
I'm on solid ground.
My feet are stable
On a rocky mound.
Lord, You are my cornerstone
As You support from Your mighty throne.

View life as your gift from God.

The Greenest View

Today is a gift called "the present,"
But do you keep wanting more?
Seeking greener grass on the other side,
A bend around the shore?

But greener and better are relative;
Life contains a degree of strife.
It takes all days as all sum up
To span your present life.

Take all days as they come.
You can't remove any single one.
Your life is a present,
God's gift to you.
Appreciate each day
With the greenest view.

Smile.

S-M-I-L-E

Smile and brighten another's bad day
When solemn eyes have so much to say.

Cheer on another when you see tears.
Another may be swallowed in fears.

Extend a hand. Extend a hug.
Say something kind and do not shrug.

Don't raise your shoulders and walk away
When you have a chance to make one's day.

Smile and brighten your own day.
Your very own eyes have so much to say.

Sprinkle needy hearts with love.

Sprinkle Overabundance

Imagine yourself carrying a watering can,
Ready to sprinkle the dry,
Where the dry are the hungry and thirsty,
Struggling to get by.

Their eyes stare with need.
Their hands outstretch for touch.
Their hearts cry for love.
Overabundance is not too much.

Imagine refilling the water can
Over and over to serve,
Being a blessed provider
For the care that others deserve.

Then turn the can toward yourself,
Sprinkling care to you,
Tending to your own needs,
For you are special too.

Awaken your sleepy soul
To each and every sense.
Rejuvenate the spirit
When it's lowly and tense.

Fill the can this time
With fragrance so sublime.
Fill the air with aromatic scents,
Fine perfumes and oils.
Reward yourself for your hard work,
All your labors and toils.

Do random acts of kindness and put someone else first.

Again and Again

Today's about you.
It's not about me.
I'll cater to you
And let you feel glee.

I'll fill your day
With acts of goodwill.
When we part,
We simply say, "Till."

Till another random day
When we will share kindness again.
This parting must not be bittersweet.
We will cater again and again.

Lead a bountiful life with generosity—giving and receiving.

The Bountiful Life

What goes around comes around,
Like reaping what you sow.
When you live your life like a circle,
Then surely you will know
How bountiful your life can be,
Filled with generosity.

With the giving you provide,
The receiving you obtain,
The reward of give and take,
How bountiful all will gain.

Realize you impact others and that many passersby impact you.

Passerby Moments

I see a familiar face.
I can't remember his or her name.
But God knows each and everyone
Who in and out of our lives came.

God has plans for us
And the people whom we meet,
From our dearest companions and friends
To the passersby on the street.

There is no way to count
The number of lives for whom you impact;
Likewise you cannot number
Those who impacted you by a special act.

The impact and influence from those who most stand out
Will be cherished remembrances that most matter and so count.

Those we hold this tight and close in mind and memory
May not even be the ones whom we regularly see.

Perhaps in a rare moment
In your young childhood,
Someone taught you a lesson
For your growing good.
Perhaps in the wink of an eye,
As you were but a teen,
Someone saw you struggling
And came to intervene.

Perhaps that notable someone was you in another's eye
When you performed a special act as a special passerby.

The Dawn of Your Personal Attitude and Conviction

This section has special meaning and message to me. I had to believe in myself. I had to keep encouraging myself step by step, word by word, page by page, and section by section. When I felt like giving up, I told myself, "I can do this. God is behind me all the way."

Seek self-encouragement and believe in yourself.

Caution to the Wind

I think I can.
I've got a plan,
So I trudge.
I let God nudge.

If the Little Engine could,
Surely so can I.
For how can I succeed,
If I never try?
Try I did,
Thought like a kid,
Inspired by the little train blue,
So loyal to his positive view.
Encouraged himself
When others said no,
The task of great pull,
The task of great tow.
As I've written on and on,
The blue engine came to mind.
Once he reached the top of the grade,
The wind he left behind.
He threw caution to the wind.
He took a risk that day
To show that he was brave and strong,
To pull others a long, long way.
When once he uttered, "I think I can,"
He changed as he rode the hill down.
"I thought I could," he uttered repetitively
As the small train of great renown.
And so it is with anything
If we set our minds to it.
Encouragement from our very own selves
Is an enterprising spirit.

Believe you can accomplish something big.

Meant for Bigger Things

You may recall a childhood story
Of a red and brave little boat,
Scuffy the Tugboat so named.
He starts in a bathtub afloat.

He tells himself, "I'm meant for bigger things,"
And soon he's lost at sea;
Whiskly and briskly sailing
On a daring adventure, so it be.

He's happy to be found and rescued
By his young boy and friend.
He doesn't mind returning to the
Bathtub 'round the bend.

This childhood tale reminds me
Of a person overwhelmed by a task,
Exerting well-meaning efforts and bearing
A frustrated look the face can't mask.

We all at one time or another
Have tried to tackle something bigger than we are.
We've felt lost on a stormy sea,
Seeking a paddle from a witness gazing from afar.

It's great to have those other eyes
Watching us sail the open sea
As we maneuver to face uncharted tasks
And territory we truly find scary.

The bigger things in life we want to secure
May challenge us on a day we've grown more mature—
To say, "I wasn't meant for smaller things but bigger things for sure!"

View life with determination.

The Potter's View

Did you ever stare at a pottery wheel
Circling 'round and 'round?
Skillful hands and watchful eye,
The artist can astound.

Your head may spin just like that wheel.
"Will I ever get it right?"
When gifted with the proper tools,
Let mind resist the fight.

For anything worth doing,
Do it right, not wrong.
Might take some trial and error.
Will you be weak or strong?

The potter takes the lump of clay,
Turns it into art.
The quitter sees an obstacle,
Not a challenge deep at heart.

The wheel is just a wheel without the potter.
The clay is just a mound without his skill.
The artist took the potter's view,
Passed a test of will.

Hardly adept when he first started,
The artist pressed on, intent and wholehearted.

If frustration spins your wheel,
The shapeless clay deformed,
Let determination rule your heart,
The quitter's view transformed.

Urge yourself to finish what you started.

Well Done

A goal is a dream waiting to happen.
When you've started, you're only half done.
For "well begun" is not the same
As hearing praises of "very well done."

Little urges can go a long way.
Encouragement will cheer you on.
When you see yourself striving,
Encourage hither and yon
To move from here to over there,
To some greater awaiting place,
To turn a dream into reality,
Touching the final base.

Like playing the game of baseball,
When you dream every hit is a home run,
Finish what you've started.
"Well done" follows "well begun."

Carry an attitude defined by your heart and inner passions.

Wherever You Go

Whoever said, "Three strikes, you're out"?
Didn't know what they were talking about.
Leave the strikeouts for a baseball park.
Adopt a new attitude to lighten the dark.
If you don't succeed, don't call it a strike.
It's a committed climb to pace a long hike.
Somehow your heart really does know
What it wants wherever you go.
Believe you can achieve
The inner passions of your heart
That don't ever go away
Yet settled there from the start.

Follow such desires that allow you to say, "What if?"

A Question of If

What if it's possible?
When?
What if it's attainable?
Then?

What if
No second doubt?
But if
Another way out?

And if
You give an excuse
As if there is no use;
Then what is your *if* that holds you back?
As if held on a board by a simple thumb tack.

Like a sticky note that just hangs there,
A reminder to act but not give due care.

If not now, then when?
If not now, when then?

Could now be your very own time
To act and not sit still?
To not let another moment pass you by,
For still is stationary will.

Will is a future tense,
Not *if* but when it transpires,
To answer your very own heart,
All it is and surely desires.

Follow such passions that allow you to look beyond and within.

Look

Look beyond the sunrise.
There lies a field of dreams,
Nestled between the mountains.
Imagination beams.
Look beyond the sunset.
There lies a river wide,
Flowing with desire.
It meets the ocean tide.
Look beyond the moon glow.
There lies a starry night.
Inspiration fills the air
Amid the bright starlight.
Look within your heart.
Discover who you are.
Find your inner passions,
The love that takes you far.

Follow the passions that carry you day by day.

Along the Way

What lies ahead are God's bright lights
Blocking our eyes from future sights.
What lies behind are lights so dimmer.
Nevertheless our pasts do shimmer.
Pasts matter and define.
But never believe your pasts confine.
Our pasts help shape who we are,
Reaffirm we've come so far.
Past days project us beyond bright lights
To grow and glow at different heights.
One day we are a star in the sky,
High above heads and every eye.
One day we are a shell by the sea,
Low in the sand where others' feet be.
Most days we're not so high or low
Beyond the lights of everyday flow.
We're just living day by day,
Following our hearts along the way.

Go through steps of loving choice—fun, happiness—and rejoice.

High and Dry

If I could blot what I have not forgot,
Such lingering pain that pours down like rain,
If I could capture and contain in a pail
Those very remnants ne'er wish to derail,
Or discard the pain to feel so freeing,
Releasing me from a captive soul being,
Then life would feel so much more fun,
As clouds no longer blockade the sun.

For I prefer the sun any day
To pouring rain that gets in my way.

I'd follow dry steps not so wet with tears.
I'd step high steps tall above fears.

For high and dry is a path of choice
To splash with happiness and feel rejoice.

The Dawn of Prayer

I opened the "Be Still the Dawn" section by drawing attention to three actions verbs:

- Ask
- Seek
- Knock

Let's sum that all up into prayer.

- Our earnest hopes and wishes
- Our solemn requests for help
- Our expressions of thanks

What "dawn" would be complete without prayer?

I wrote the following personal prayer one day as I meditated by the shoreline. I repeat it often, as it is very much ingrained in my heart and mind.

My Serenity Prayer

God, grant me a tranquil mind,
Like the low tides of the ocean,
A constant ebb and flow
To surf the high tides of emotion.
Lord, give me a patient spirit
That is kind and persevering,
A humble and courageous heart
With a rhythm so endearing.

Unite faith and hope.

Ever So Tight

Hold on to faith here and now
When you feel sweat from brow to brow.
Carry on with hope forward each day
As once-pressing sweat held you at bay.
Experience freedom beyond drowning sweat.
Ask God in prayer to dry all your fret.
Sweat and fret may closely unite,
But faith and hope are ever so tight.

Ask others to pray for you.

From Head to Toe

Do me a favor when I feel woe.
Pray for me from head to toe.
My head may wander,
My eyes overlook
Simple answers
That I mistook.
My heart may waver
Or even flutter.
My voice may quiver
Or even stutter.
My knees may cave,
And that's okay
To fall in prayer
When feeling dismay.
My feet may be still.
My toes may feel numb.
Then finally,
I may succumb
To greater strength:
The Lord, our provider,
Comforter, friend,
Loving confider.
To greater power
Beyond my will,
I will rise again.
My feet won't be still.

Hear prayers answered.

The Nomad and His Husky

The nomad approached a fork in the road.
It looked like an overturned *T*.
"Should we go straight or left or right?"
He asked his companion, a husky.

The husky barked and pulled to the left.
The nomad scratched his head.
The nomad paused and tugged on the leash.
"Let's go to the right instead."

The nomad took a few steps right.
The husky lay down at his feet.
The nomad scratched his head again.
"Let's opt to walk the straight street."

The dog arose with a discerning sense.
The nomad followed behind.
In a matter of speaking,
Was the blind leading the blind?

The nomad and his dog were blind to what lay ahead,
But they chose the straight road in search of a glorious homestead.

The nomad and his companion walked many miles so straight.
Up ahead in front of them sat a chapel behind a gate.

The nomad and his husky did not hesitate.
Though tired and so weary, they sped toward that gate.

The nomad fell to his knees and prayed at the chapel door.
He prayed they'd chosen the straight road and vowed to veer no more.

The chapel they knelt before was a homestead filled with glory.
The nomad and his husky found the Lord's house in their story.

Kneel to pray at church altars.

Chosen

Church dome, call me home.
Church spire, so inspire.
Call me to walk the track by the pews
To the beautiful altar I choose.
To kneel and pray; quiet moments I stay
To cry, to talk, to close my eyes;
To feel, to heal, and so then to rise.
The dome and spire will call me back
To kneel and pray at the "chosen" track.

Above all, forgive as our Lord's Prayer teaches.

The Rose-Colored Rule

Admit when wounded deep or slight,
Then forgive with all your might.

Forgive as many times as it takes
And treasure relationships that you do make.

The Dawn of the Staircase to Heaven

On some serene day when you are feeling so at peace, you might look into the sky and see a staircase. Perhaps you'll find a ladder that reaches high into parting puffy, white clouds.

Fairest Vision

Lily of the valley white,
Pure and lovely in my sight.

Lily in the valley green,
Fairest flower I have seen.

Rose of Sharon, crimson red,
Bold and vivid in the lily bed,
Stands alone in the field of white,
Effervescent, glowing bright.

Illuminating the way to heaven's staircase,
A heavenly ladder before thy face.

Rising upward toward the sky,
Each rung is Jesus, the Way so high.

The ladder glows against sky pale blue
To those who see it, standing true.

So firmly from fertile land so green,
Fairest vision I have seen.

Find a towering ladder to a greater homestead.

A Chateau and a Ladder

High above the mountaintop,
I gaze from a lofty plateau.
I see rolling fields, lush and green,
And the rooftop of a single chateau.

The little house that sits alone,
Unoccupied, yet still a throne.

Once inhabited by a mighty scribe,
He lived a life I must describe.

He dwelt down low but lived up high.
His passions pointed far to the sky.

God made the soil below his feet,
But he wanted more than just a seat.

God made the sky above his head
Like a towering ladder to a greater homestead.

For the scribe saw heaven in the sky,
A royal chateau sparkling in his eye.

A chateau grander than his valley's estate,
His future home at the pearly gate.

The scribe turned ninety, and at that age,
He passed and turned a life's new page.

A physical life he'd have no more
Not upon this earth.
But spiritually, he'd find his throne
And be crowned a newfound birth.

The Dawn of Heaven—A Love's Ascent

One day, we will each be called to a greater home. And that home becomes our greatest dawn, ... a celestial home.

The Dove Ascends

May I feel like a graceful bird released into the sky,
Like a swift and pure white dove whose wings will get her by.

Whose wings will carry her between sky and land,
Knowing there's waiting a patient hand.

The hand of God to catch her, if ever she should fall;
Comparatively speaking, she is so very small.

Small and fragile yet mighty in flight;
Most at home at celestial height.

In this world, she will soulfully ascend;
Not of this world, we can't pretend.

We are to love heaven more than earth,
Where God so gave life to all since birth.

Promise awaits.

Grace

Happy places.
Smiling faces.
Warm embraces.
Loving graces.
Footsteps leaving traces
Of where our lives have been,
On a journey to be saved
And forgiven of all sin.
Heaven promises all,
And so it one day awaits
Until that time be thankful
For all your fortunes and fates.

An eternal home awaits.

Home

Lord, remove the roam
So I may find a home.
Though temporary upon this earth,
Home is home until rebirth.
The day I see a pearly gate
That I walk through with steady gait.

Peace will be with you.

Walk in Peace

May you walk in peace
And know it's dawn,
Entering God's palace
Like a newborn fawn.
So light on your feet,
Could be swept like a feather.
You graciously sashay
Through berries and heather.
Let the trumpets sound.
The choirs sing out.
Doves soar from the ground
As the angels do shout.

Paradise will awaken you.

Life on the Paradise Side

Let us be reminded that life awakens anew.
New pages and chapters will unfold.
For those who loved us earlier in life,
We have memories to cherish and behold.

Your loved ones would want no more
Than for you to be happy for your life in store.

To look at each day as a brand-new dawn,
Heaven's gates one day shall open wide
When it is your time to receive God's free gift
Of eternal life on the paradise side.

As we near the end of this memoir, I have threaded poems with caption text to tell an even larger story. I have sewn a quilt for you. Always remember: a quilt tells a story.

A Patchwork Quilt

When life feels torn like jagged patches,
Broken glass with chips and scratches,
Darkness feels settling like invisible night,
But brokenness is where we see light.
Thence, I choose to honor those breaks
And sew a quilt to lighten those aches.

My quilt, my story, my life so told.
More dreams and hurts will surely enfold.
My blanket will grow bigger and bigger each day,
A hope that my knitting is led by God's way.

Grass of brown patches where reeds have so died,
Quilted together, each patch I so cried.
A blanket of tears so woefully sewn,
Each heartfelt pain that I've ever known.
Each heartfelt joy forms a patchwork of green,
Beautiful grass alive in between.
Times of happiness, love, and cheer
Embedded in patches sweet and so dear.

Likewise, if you would sew your frame,
No two quilts would look the same.
Your story would be a growing blend too
Of patches you lived, how God saw you through.
For each of us has been enlightened
With awareness and outlook so heightened.
Each and every quilt and story
Is a gift of life and its glory.

Jesus	**K**	*Jesus*
	N	
G	**O**	**D**
	W	
	I	
	N	
Jesus	**G**	*Jesus*

The three-by-seven visual I used in "Be Still and Know" is now stitched into the quilt displayed to the left. Let Jesus be your cornerstone for all boundaries. To get to God, you must go through Jesus. We see light at all edges to draw our attention to the center: the cross. Our all-knowing God wants you to know Him. May God and Jesus guide you as you quilt your story, your life.

Thank you, Lord, for placing these messages in my heart to share with and inspire others. This has truly been a fruitful experience to be a branch to reach others and to speak of God's wonders.

As you journey forward, remember a spiritual life is about knowing God and Jesus and bearing fruit. As you feel restored through God's grace, think of "dawn" as a state of fruition. "Fruition" is realization and a state of accomplishment and reality. Fruition is derived from the Latin *frui*. "Frui" means to enjoy.

You are a branch. Reach out and reach further. Enjoy bearing fruit and feeling a sense of union with God.

John 15:1 says, "I am the true vine, and my Father is the gardener."

Fruition is bearing fruit that glorifies our gardener. God is pleased as His children grow in the nine characteristics of the fruit of the spirit.

Galatians 5:22-25 says, "But the fruit of the Spirit is love, joy, peace, forbearance, kindness, goodness, faithfulness, gentleness and self-control. Against such things there is no law. Those who belong to Christ Jesus have crucified the flesh with its passions and desires. Since we live by the Spirit, let us keep in step with the Spirit."

At the onset of this memoir, I stated that I chose 333 odes for Jesus. He died at age 33 and delivered the most powerful message. Jesus died so that we may have life and be saved. Jesus desires that we accept God's word, much like rich soil nourishes a seed for growth. Notice the meaningful parallelism in the following Bible verses.

Luke 8:14-15 says, "The seed that fell among thorns stands for those who hear, but as they go on their way they are choked by life's worries, riches and pleasures, and they do not mature. But the seed on good soil stands for those with a noble and good heart, who hear the word, retain it, and by persevering produce a crop."

In a dawning moment, relish in spiritual fruitfulness. God wants us to be fertile and to produce like good soil. From this foundation, we allow our inner fruits to mature. We do good works and deeds with and for others. We help others as they grow and let their inner fruits blossom and shine. We glorify God with our words and actions. We transform and feel restored. Reality changes as we allow ourselves to perpetually grow.

As you journey with steps of faith, may you realize to live a Christian life is to walk constantly with the fruit of the spirit. You will have days you feel like a barren twig. You will have days you feel like a leafy, green branch so nurtured and full of life. Grow and rise high like a tree. Aspire to live like Jesus, the perfect fruit. Be guided by this Bible verse as you shape your life to be more like Jesus.

John 15:16 says, "You did not choose me, but I chose you and appointed you so that you might go and bear fruit—fruit that will last—and so that whatever you ask in my name the Father will give you."

Remember these three lines as you think about Jesus. Let them be your *3 for 33*.

The fruit we bear today sows seeds for tomorrow. Those seeds bear more fruit. Capture the first light of day as the sun rises at dawn, and watch the sun set each dusk knowing that day produced fruition.

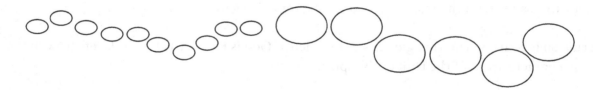

Thank you, my readers, for journeying with me through this poetic memoir.

May

May you always remember there's no destination to go
But to experience life's journey like the sea's ebb and flow.
May you walk hand in hand with those you love.
May you never forget that your guider is above.
May you be a follower and disciple to God's ways.
God loves you, and I do too, now and ever always.

We come to a close of *Be Still the Dawn*. This ode introduces the heartfelt poem that provided me the vision for this book. Imagine its author sitting at a desk, freshly typing this poem and whispering.

Poem Not Forgotten

As the poet in me stares at a blank page
To emotionally compose a rhyme,
To introduce *Be Still the Dawn*
Like a page torn out of time.

Where did the original poem go?
I will tell you now.
Now's the time as the book comes to close,
So I want you to know how.

Written for Dad's mother, who before him
Departed this earth in April that year;
The following year was Dad's time to meet God.
He left us to join my grandmother dear.

Lonely and sad without her,
Grief shone on his face.
The day he finally departed,
He left with my words as an embrace.

I'll take a moment to chat with Dad
And will now address him as "You."
To think back to that moment
When I was lonely and sad too.

"When You rose to the skies above,
Inside your pocket there it be;
Be Still the Dawn, the poem—
For You to take with thee."

As I so folded it carefully,
Tucked it safely so.
Looked at You to say, "Good-bye,"
And I didn't want to turn and go.

"Maybe through You,
I was bestowed this gift
To put words into poems
For souls to uplift.

I have had no greater glory or honor
Than to praise You, Dad, with loving honor.
And I have cherished the joy and time
To praise our God through my book of rhyme."

Now I stare at the closing poem,
The words brought back in time.
My heart is so illuminated by
My devoted verse and rhyme.

Be Still the Dawn

The day breaks.
The night falls.
The sun rises.
The moon calls.

The stars above.
The ground below.
The mountain high.
The river flow.

The eyes shimmer
The ocean tide.
The flower blooms
The smile so wide.

The mind recalls
The memory old.
The feeling new
The heart unfold.

A message here
With words so true.
Be Still the Dawn
With love to you.

Epilogue

Since completing the first draft of this memoir, I experienced such a divine connection that I want to share additional words. I want to share a beautiful autumn morning … a vision of inner peace.

The following story is poetic and not one of the original 333 "ode-votionals." This closing section reflects my afterthoughts. This is what makes writing interesting and creative, … choosing to include the unexpected. I have left this additional blessing untitled so you may define a title you find personally fitting.

It was a beautiful, crisp autumn morning.
I saw trees of yellow, orange, and red.
My heart weighed so heavily that day
As thoughts seared and turned in my head.

I drove to the cemetery,
Inside feeling ever so sad.
This day felt like a calling, a quest—
To read to my grandparents and Dad.

I worked so hard on *Be Still the Dawn*.
I had so much to say.
"Look, look, hear, hear
What more I have to say."

I could not contain my thoughts.
My expressions were genuine and real.
I read several verses of poetry
As if I wanted to make them feel.

I sat down by the tombstone on one side,
Read contently so.
I moved around to the other side.
I read "Be Still and Know."

I only chose a few poems
To read with heartfelt depth.
My tears soon started to flow,
And it was there alone I wept.

I treasured that alone time
More than you'll ever know.
I may have been just one body there,
But in spirit there was more, I know.

It was just that magical feeling
As if I were being heard
With each and every utterance,
As I spoke rhyme and verse and word.

It was such a divine connection
That will remain captured in my heart,
As well as in my memories
As I go forward and depart.

I knew I couldn't stay all day.
The preciousness was found in moments.
I know I will return on another fine day
When preciousness will shine in mere moments.

Psalm 46:10 says, "He says, 'Be still, and know that I am God; I will be exalted among the nations, I will be exalted in the earth.'"

Printed in the United States
By Bookmasters